When Your Best
Isn't Good
Enough

Other books by Dr. Kevin Leman

Making Children Mind without Losing Yours
My Firstborn, There's No One Like You
My Middle Child, There's No One Like You
My Youngest, There's No One Like You
My Only Child, There's No One Like You
The Birth Order Book
Be Your Own Shrink
Pleasers
First-Time Mom
A Chicken's Guide to Talking Turkey to Your Kids about Sex
The Way of the Shepherd
The Perfect Match
Sheet Music
Sex Begins in the Kitchen
Running the Rapids
Say Good-bye to Stress
Keeping Your Family Strong in a World Gone Wrong
What a Difference a Daddy Makes
Becoming a Couple of Promise
Women Who Try Too Hard
Becoming the Parent God Wants You to Be

Video Series

Making Children Mind without Losing Yours
Making the Most of Marriage
Single Parenting That Works!
Bringing Peace and Harmony to the Blended Family

When Your Best Isn't Good Enough

The Secret of Measuring Up

Dr. Kevin Leman

Revell
Grand Rapids, Michigan

© 1988, 2007 by Kevin Leman

Published by Fleming H. Revell
a division of Baker Publishing Group
P.O. Box 6287, Grand Rapids, MI 49516-6287
www.revellbooks.com

New paperback edition published 2007
ISBN 10: 0-8007-3193-X
ISBN 978-0-8007-3193-9

Previously published in 1988 under the title *Measuring Up* and in 1997 under the title *When Your Best Is Not Good Enough*

Printed in the United States of America

The Library of Congress has cataloged the previous edition as follows:
Leman, Kevin.
    [Measuring up]
    When your best is not good enough : the secret of measuring up /
Kevin Leman.
        p.   cm.
    Originally published: Measuring up. Old Tappan, N.J.: Revell, c1988.
    Includes bibliographical references.
    ISBN 10: 0-8007-5636-3 (pbk.)
    ISBN 978-0-8007-5636-9 (pbk.)
    1. Self-doubt. 2. Failure (Psychology) 3. Perfectionism (Personality trait) 4. Expectation (Psychology) 5. Self-perception. I. Title.
[BF697.5.S428L46 1997]
158.1—dc21   95-25997

In keeping with biblical principles of creation stewardship, Baker Publishing Group advocates the responsible use of our natural resources. As a member of the Green Press Initiative, our company uses recycled paper when possible. The text paper of this book is comprised of 30% post-consumer waste.

green press INITIATIVE

To
my son,
Kevin Anderson Leman II

Your humor, sensitivity, and concern for others
make us proud to be your mom and dad.
Mom and I love you very much.

Contents

Introduction   9

Part 1 Starting Out on the Wrong Foot

1. Why Can't I Measure Up?   13
2. What's This Thing Called *Life-Style*?   21
3. How the Pattern Begins: The Early Years   39

Part 2 Discovering Who You Really Are

4. The Critical Parent and You   93
5. The Problem with Guilt   123
6. Is It Time to Lower Your High-Jump Bar of Life?   151
7. Help and Healing for Your Broken Heart   201

Part 3 No Losers in the Game of Life

8. A Few People Who Didn't Measure Up   221
9. It's Great Being You!   235

Notes   251

Introduction

After writing *The Birth Order Book* in 1985, I got an avalanche of responses to one specific part of that bestselling book. I talked about a syndrome that I observed in people over and over again: *perfectionism*.

Perhaps you know this person. He or she starts a lot of projects and doesn't finish them. Their motto is, "If I can put it off for a day (or a year) or two, all the better." If you look on their desk at their place of work, you'll see signs of the defeated perfectionist—they live in piles. If you ask these people to find something on their cluttered desks, they'll find it with ease. If you want to send them into a tizzy, move their piles. There is order within the disorder.

But these personality types have a unique way of defeating themselves. Let's look at a student who fits the profile. This young person needs to study for a final exam. He tells himself throughout the day that he is going to study all night. Evening arrives, and he sits down to bury himself in his books, only to find himself studying for just a few minutes before seeing that shirt or that jacket that needs to be hung up across the room. What's the probability of him returning to his studies? Zero?

Nada? Zilch? Bingo! You should have been a psychologist. This syndrome is produced in people who are brought up with at least one critical-eyed parent. That parent can spot a flaw at forty paces. And these personalities protect themselves from criticism by simply not completing tasks and not performing up to their abilities.

So, because of the overwhelming response, I wrote the book *When Your Best Isn't Good Enough*. It's intended to help those afflicted with this syndrome to remove the high-jump bar of life that seems to stymie them at every turn.

My hope is that it will help you.

Part 1

Starting Out
on the Wrong Foot

1

Why Can't I Measure Up?

You're bound to know the feeling.

Maybe it only comes around at family reunions, when you see your younger brother, Fred, again. There he is—tan, handsome, athletic—and a tremendous success in the world of business.

Most of the time you're pretty self-confident. You're doing okay in the world, and your friends seem to like and respect you.

But then, there *he* is—and all of a sudden you feel like you're six years old again, with torn pants and a dirty face. You suddenly realize that whatever you've done with your life, it hasn't been enough. No matter how much you know, it isn't as much as he knows.

No, sir. You couldn't measure up to this magnificent brother when you were a kid—and you're still standing in his shadow. You feel so . . . so . . . inadequate. At any minute he's bound to come up and tell you that you have spinach stuck between your teeth, or that your fly's open. Maybe you'd better stay over here, in the corner.

If it isn't your brother who brings out these feelings in you, perhaps it's somebody like *her* . . . Mary Johnson, who still looks terrific after all these years.

You had to practically starve yourself for six weeks to get down to a size 12 for your high school reunion. And then she shows up wearing a stunning size 5! And just look at that figure!

If situations such as these are the only times you feel like something of a failure, then you can consider yourself very lucky. You've developed a pretty healthy self-image.

Many people—no matter what they may say or how they may conduct themselves—really don't feel very good about themselves. They feel inadequate, like failures and rejects much of the time. And they're not. They're ordinary, productive citizens, who have just never been able to feel they measure up. They try so hard, but always seem to come up short. Even when they succeed, they feel as if they just got lucky, or that they've failed.

They don't measure up to their parents' expectations, their teachers' expectations, or even their own expectations. They always feel as if they've let somebody down, and in many instances they have become so defeated and weary that they live out their lives in a way that reinforces their opinion of themselves. These people are defeated perfectionists. Defeated because they can never clear what I call "the high-jump bar of life."

If they ever do manage to get over it, they quickly raise it up a notch or two so they can never get over it a second time.

In my more than thirty years of private psychological practice I've talked to thousands of these people, and I've come to see consistent patterns of thought and actions—patterns that reinforce the "I just can't measure up" syndrome.

I don't care who you are, or what has happened in your life up to this point. You are not a failure, and you do not have to live your life as one.

This book is being written to help everyone who has ever struggled with feelings of self-doubt and inadequacy, no matter how strong and consistent or weak and sporadic those feelings may be. I want to help you break the cycle of failure and rejection. I want to teach parents how to instill a positive self-image in their children. And I want to help you understand how you got caught in this vicious cycle in the first place. The defeated perfectionist can be set free from discouragement and failure, and I'll show you how.

Now, I've already told you that I'm a psychologist, and that I've counseled thousands of people over the past thirty years. But don't think for a moment that I'm going to approach the subject with the cold and detached eye of a clinician. I'm not going to be writing from some lofty ivory tower and use only words you might find in the *Reader's Digest* under "It Pays to Enrich Your Word Power."

I haven't always been a psychologist, and I wasn't born with a doctorate degree. When I write about the feeling of not being able to measure up, believe me, I know what I'm talking about.

For instance, when you hear the word *undistinguished* you might as well think of my high school career. I graduated a "gimme putt" from the bottom of my class. I was in a reading group in elementary school where one kid ate paste and two others continually smiled for no apparent reasons. I was a college dropout who worked for a while as a janitor in a hospital. The head nurse there took my future wife, Sande, aside and told her not to go out with me because it was clear I was never going to amount to anything, and that she was wasting her time with the likes of me. (I'll tell you more about this later.)

And I'll have to admit, at the time that looked like some pretty good advice. (But I'm awfully glad Sande didn't take it!)

Take It from One Who Knows

What's my point? Only that I know what I'm talking about not only on the professional level, but on the personal level as well. When you're starting out on a vacation trip, it's one thing to look at all the colorful brochures and believe what they say. It's another thing to take the advice of someone who knows where you should stay because he's been there himself. Well . . . I've been there!

I'll talk more about that later on, but before we go further I want to assure you of something else: People who see themselves as not being able to measure up are often some of the most intelligent, attractive, and productive people around. If you're one of those who are troubled with thoughts of inadequacy you're in some pretty good company.

I remember Joanne, for instance, who was warm, intelligent, and absolutely beautiful, with soft golden hair, Carolina blue eyes, and a perfect smile. It was hard to find the slightest flaw on that face, and the rest of her was not bad either!

She was the sort of woman who couldn't walk into a crowded room without causing several male heads to turn in her direction. Her looks, coupled with her sparkling personality, made her a most-eligible and sought-after young woman.

But she never saw any of that, and her charming personality was only a front. Beneath the surface she was miserable, sad, and lonely; she considered herself to be a terrible failure.

She wanted desperately to find a man to love her—or at least she thought she did. But even though she had many "relationships," they always ended in disaster.

The truth was that Joanne, like many others I have counseled, was caught up in the self-perpetuating cycle of not being able to measure up.

She unconsciously sabotaged every one of those relationships because she had grown so used to living in a world of broken dreams.

It could be that this is what has happened in your life. You have come, for whatever reason, to see yourself as someone whose best efforts are bound to fail. You just can't seem to get your life into sync.

You're the type of person who puts his life savings into the stock market, two days before Black Friday. You go to buy a house and the interest rates quickly jump two percentage points. You go to sell a house and a subdivision with three thousand units opens its doors just across the street.

Sometimes you don't know whether to laugh or cry, and you often feel like doing both at the same time. It doesn't matter how strong you are. Sometimes all it takes to get things rolling in the wrong direction is one or two setbacks. We begin to see ourselves as "losers"—or at the least we begin to think that some mystical forces are aligned against us, so we might as well be resigned to lives of defeat and futility.

That, in essence, is what had happened to Joanne. And she had to come to see that there were no real obstacles standing in the way of her lasting happiness—only her own decisions and choices based on the way she subconsciously perceived herself.

I remember Jim, a good-looking athletic man in his mid-thirties. He was intelligent and successful in the world of business.

Jim had been married, once, but it had lasted less than five years, and since then he'd had a succession of unsuccessful relationships. He was no playboy, either. He wanted desperately to find a woman with whom he could share his life. He loved children and wanted to have a family, and it scared him to find that he was still alone with "no prospects" at thirty-seven.

He was just like Joanne. Everyone around him saw him as successful and self-assured, but he had come to believe, at a very early age, that he simply did not measure up. So he punished himself by rejecting anyone who really began to care about him. Commitment wasn't a word in Jim's vocabulary. He had hurt several women deeply, but what they didn't understand was that he broke off relationships not because he was rejecting them, but because he was rejecting himself. He could never measure up to their expectations.

Again, that wasn't a conscious decision he made. He would always find some reason to terminate the relationship—most of them quite petty. He would suddenly discover that he didn't like the way Judi laughed, or the way Donna slurped her soup, and that would be the end of the relationship.

The truth was, though, that he was never the one to "officially" terminate things. He would just begin finding fault, nagging, and criticizing until his women friends got the picture and decided to break things off. In this way, he was always the one being rejected instead of the one doing the rejecting.

Jim's problem was not only that he felt he could not measure up, but that he had come to believe, as a young child, that the only way he could really get the attention he craved was to be rejected. It was not an easy task to get him to see that he was a worthwhile human being, that he had much to bring to any relationship, and that he, himself, was bringing about his own rejection.

Joanne and Jim acted similarly for different reasons, and I'll be talking more about those reasons later on. But they stand out in my mind as two dramatic examples of people who were failing in the most important area of life—the search for love and companionship—not because they were unattractive or unworthy, but because they had both come to believe that they did not, could not, and would never measure up to that impossible standard by which they evaluated their own self-worth.

You may not be a stunning beauty like Joanne, nor a six-two "hunk" like Jim. And I certainly don't bring them up so you'll compare yourself to them. My purpose, rather, is to show that feelings of unworthiness and rejection seldom have any basis in reality.

You're Wrong about Yourself

Do you consider yourself to be a failure?

Well, you're wrong, and I hope that by the time you finish reading this book you will come to see how you fell into the

18

"I-just-can't-measure-up" trap, and, more important, what you can do to find your way out of it. Because you can be set free from the cycle of rejection and failure.

And it's about time you had the joy of discovering the truth about yourself—that you have everything you need to come out a winner in this game called life!

Are You a Defeated Perfectionist?

Here's a brief quiz to help you find out.

1. If your boss asks you to do a special report for him, would you be most likely to:
   A. Immediately be afraid you'd never get it finished by his deadline?
   B. Worry about whether he'd like your finished project?
   C. Be proud of the fact that the boss had chosen you?
2. If you called your best friend on the phone and he asked you to please call back later because he was late for an appointment, would you:
   A. Think you had offended him somehow and he simply didn't want to talk to you?
   B. Felt that this was typical, because everything else was more important to him than you are?
   C. Gladly agree to call him back, and think nothing further about it?
3. If you overslept and were fifteen minutes late for work, would you:
   A. Figure that your reputation was ruined because everyone had seen you coming in late?
   B. Report yourself to the boss and promise to work thirty minutes of your lunch hour to make up for it?
   C. Realize that everyone oversleeps once in a while, and promise yourself that you'll try not to do it again?

In all of the questions, the A and B answers are normal routine for the defeated perfectionists. Only the C answers show a healthy sense of self-esteem.

Question No. 1: Defeated perfectionists are excellent when it comes to contemplating disaster and failure.

Question No. 2: They're also great at seeing rejection and criticism everywhere.

Question No. 3: Another favorite pastime of the defeated perfectionist is magnifying his mistakes and flaws.[1]

2

What's This Thing Called *Life-Style?*

On first glance you know that Betty and Rhonda are sisters. They *have* to be because they look so much alike. And if you closed your eyes and just listened to them talking, you wouldn't know which one was saying what. Even their voices seem the same.

But once you get to know them, you realize that you must have been mistaken. They may look alike and sound alike, but they certainly don't act alike—and there's just no way the two of them could come from the same family!

Betty, for instance, has made a tremendous success of her life, and you can be sure of that just by looking at her. She dresses with impeccable taste, looks like she just stepped off the cover of *Redbook* magazine, and she stands tall and erect. She doesn't seem arrogant, but there is a certain pride about her, something that says she believes in herself. She's been with the same company for fifteen years and recently earned the title of vice-president.

Her marriage is a success, too, as she's been able to balance the twin careers of business executive and wife/mother. She's been married to the same man for thirteen years, and she and her husband are the proud parents of three well-behaved children.

No doubt about it—Betty is one of the most "together" women you've ever met.

So what happened to Rhonda?

While Betty stands tall and erect, Rhonda stands slouched and scrunched up like an accordion. Her posture says that she doesn't respect herself very much, and her wardrobe—ill-fitting, mismatched clothes—certainly confirms that impression. Rhonda is every bit as intelligent as Betty, but for some reason she's never been able to do anything with her life. She's drifted from job to job, never able to hold on to one for more than a year or two, and she's been divorced twice. Since her last marriage ended she's drifted in and out of relationships. She'd like to find a man to be her lifelong companion, but she's just about resigned herself to the fact that it will never happen.

No, sir. Betty and Rhonda might look alike, but there's just no way they could be sisters.

But they are! Women who grew up in the same family and are only two years apart in age, they attended the same schools, the same synagogue, enjoyed the same opportunities in life. So what happened?

Why has Betty made something out of her life, while Rhonda is always getting herself into financial difficulty and calling on her sister to bail her out?

The answer to this question is that each of these sisters is following her own particular *life-style*. This doesn't mean that Betty sat down at some point and drew up a plan for her life which included success in business and a happy marriage. Nor does it mean that Rhonda has chosen to be somewhat less than a success.

What it does mean, though, is that both of these women are following definite plans for their lives—plans that were developed early in their childhoods. The things they do, the choices they make, are determined by the life-styles they are following—albeit subconsciously.

What exactly is a *life-style*? Basically, it is a concept developed by the pioneer psychologist Alfred Adler. Adler believed that understanding a person's goals is a key to understanding a person's behavior. He believed that all of us are following individual "life lines" or paths toward specific goals. Everything we do is oriented toward some goal, whether or not we understand what that goal is.[1]

When considering why someone never seems to measure up, it's important to take a look at the factors that enter into the makeup of his life-style. Many people, for various reasons, are following life-styles that are bound up in cycles of rejection and failure—and we'll discuss some of these reasons as we go along.[2]

Attacking the Roots of Rejection

It is important for anyone who feels as if he can't measure up to get at the roots of the matter—to examine his life-style and discover how and why this continuous cycle of "unworthiness" got started. Once that is understood, the next step is to realize that life patterns can be changed, and that new, constructive attitudes and actions can be put in place of the old.

You've undoubtedly heard the old saying "You can't teach an old dog new tricks." Well, that's not quite true, but it is harder to redefine and reshape the life-style once a person has reached adolescence. Personality is like wet cement up until age seven, then it gets progressively harder. Your life-style is so deeply ingrained into your personality by the time you're, say, fourteen that it's hardened to the point where you could roller-skate on

23

it. But even then, there are steps you can take to change your life-style.

For the most part, your life-style is a product of your environment. It consists of the way you perceive yourself in relationship to the significant people around you. All men and women follow certain life-styles, which may be positive or negative. There are the controllers, the pleasers, attention-getters, victims, perfectionists, winners, and so on, all of them following patterns that were established early in life.

Okay, I hear what you're saying: "If the life-style I follow comes as a result of the environment of my early years, then what in the world happened to Betty and Rhonda? They're sisters, so aren't they products of the same environment?"

No, not at all.

Each child in a family can be considered to be living in a different environment, and so each life-style will be influenced by different factors. The family environment changes with the birth of each child.

For example, Betty was the oldest child, the apple of her parents' eyes, who always did well in school and never did anything to cause her mom and dad to be embarrassed.

Rhonda, on the other hand, was the perpetual little sister, the one who always stood in Betty's shadow and could never do anything—or so it seemed—as well as big sister could do it. If Rhonda came home from school with the good news that she had received a *B* in math, she was reminded that Betty never made anything less than an *A*. If she got a few lines in the school play, she was reminded that her sister had won the lead. And so it went.

Betty's environment was shaped by her role as the "golden child" of the family, whereas Rhonda was a frustrated underachiever, who soon resigned herself to the fact that she would never measure up to her sister. True to her expectations about herself, she never has. Both girls grew up, then, in totally different atmospheres which shaped the way they will see themselves and live out their lives forever—unless Rhonda sees that she does not have to be trapped in her life-style of failure and chooses to do something about it.

In Rhonda's case, though, the situation was compounded by the fact that the only time she ever brought any attention to herself was when she failed. Most of the time, she felt as if her parents had forgotten she existed. But every once in a while, when she had tried—and failed—to measure up to something her sister had done, her mother would take her in her arms and comfort her.

It wasn't too long before she discovered that failure had its rewards, and she would stop trying so hard to measure up to her sister, realizing that her shortcomings at least got her some attention. It wasn't that she really tried to fail—at least not consciously—but her subconscious was working overtime to get her some attention any way it could! Once she had learned that failure was a good way, at least, to have her moment in the spotlight, she began to fail more and more. Her failures, her never measuring up to anyone's expectations, were a deeply ingrained part of her personality.

Don't get me wrong, Rhonda didn't *want* to fail. She didn't enjoy being fired from jobs or seeing her marriages go down the drain—but her life-style had led her into a pattern of failure from which it seemed there would be no escape.

The more years I spend as a psychologist, the more I am convinced of the truth of that old saying "As the twig is bent, so grows the tree."

The things that happen to us very early in life will shape the way we live out the rest of our years. Even if they live to be 120, most people will be following the life-style that was built into them by the time they were four or five years old.

As the Twig Is Bent . . .

When I began analyzing a patient's life-style, one of the first questions I ask is, "What is your earliest childhood memory?"

It's amazing how often that first memory can give insight into a person's overall life-style. That first memory, selected from among hundreds of other early incidents, is an excellent indicator of how we looked at life. Whereas there are thousands of incidents that happen to all of us in our earliest years, we tend to remember most clearly those that are consistent with how we see ourselves in relationship to others.

What is your first memory? Do you remember being embarrassed and ashamed because you had done something wrong? Perhaps you had wet your pants in front of the other kids and they were laughing at you? Or do you remember your father taking you on his lap and telling you that the drawing you just made was a wonderful work of art?

There isn't a person alive who hasn't done something embarrassing at one time or another and found himself the subject of derisive laughter. And there aren't too many who haven't experienced at least a few victories. But if you center on the embarrassments and the mistakes, you may be following a life-style that leads to further rejection and humiliation. If, on the other hand, you are a person who tends to forget the embarrassments altogether, and focus on the times you did well and made others proud of you, your life-style will be one of healthy self-respect. And a major key toward success in life is self-respect.

Now this doesn't mean that every child in the same set of circumstances will develop the same life-style. It's a matter of what the child does with those circumstances, how he perceives his role as an individual.

Consider two families with handicapped children. Both Sheila and Sherri are confined to wheelchairs, and doctors say that neither one of them will ever be able to walk.

Sheila's family reacts to her handicap by doing everything they can for her. They protect and coddle her, making excuses for her because of her handicap. In this way they are, in fact, rejecting her, telling her that she is a lesser person because she can't walk. In their attempts to help her, they are, instead, harming her, and seeing to it that her life-style will be one of dependency on others and of never measuring up.

Sherri's parents have the opposite reaction. They realize that there are some things their daughter can't do for herself, and they help her as much as is absolutely necessary. But at the same time, they take pains to see that in most ways she is treated the same as their other children. Their attitude is, "Yes, you have a handicap, but you shouldn't let it hold you back." They always challenge her, within reason, to do things for herself, and she is not pitied nor babied.

Sherri, even though her physical handicap is every bit as limiting as Sheila's, will develop a "can-do" life-style. She will respect herself and her abilities and is not likely to allow her physical disability to control her entire life.

So you see there are many forces that go into the development of a life-style. If someone has developed a "defeated perfectionist" life-style and feels as if he can't ever measure up, the fault does not lie entirely with parents, or siblings, or the family's financial circumstances. These are all factors that come into play in the development of a personality, and it is not always easy to uncover the reasons for development of such a life-style.

The important thing, though, is to realize that we are all following very definite life-style patterns and that, with patience, hard work, and understanding, a life-style can be altered.

But again, unless there is some intervention, the life-styles we develop as very young children will stay with us throughout our lives.

If Johnny is a perfectionist when he's five, chances are that he'll still be a perfectionist when he's forty.

If Mary's a show-off at five, she'll probably still be trying to hog the limelight when she's thirty-five.

If Joey is a shy child, who feels that he can't do anything right, it's highly likely that he'll still be doing his best to stay in the background, to avoid being compared with others, when he's fifty.

Have you ever known anyone who was a chronic complainer? I have. You know, most of the time, when someone says to us, "Hello, how are you?" we don't think twice before answering, "Fine, thanks, and you?"

Most of us could be walking down the street with arrows sticking out of our backs and we'd still say, "Fine, thanks, and you?"

I mean, how would you feel if you said to someone, "How ya doin' today?" and he said, "To tell you the truth, my hemorrhoids are killing me"?

You'd think the guy was crazy, to say the least. Quite frankly, you weren't that interested.

But not Martha Martyr. She was the type of woman who, when you asked her how she was doing, would not hesitate to tell you—and she was never, ever doing "fine." She would spare no detail while telling you every single thing that was wrong with her, and there were always so many things wrong that I half expected, at any moment, to see her actually crumble into a little heap of sawdust.

The first few times I spoke to her I made the same mistake: "How are you today?"

"Well, let me tell you, Dr. Leman . . ." and then she was off to the races. I half suspected she used to watch doctor shows on television just to find new ailments she could develop.

Finally, I learned my lesson. "Hello," was fine. "It's good to see you," was marvelous. But I learned to avoid those magic words, "How are you today?" Of course, it didn't really matter, because she was bound and determined to tell me—whether or not I asked. Martha was not a client of mine, nor was she interested in changing her behavior.

I bring her up merely to point out how a person's life-style can affect his life. Martha had undoubtedly learned, while a very little girl, that she received attention only when she was injured. If she fell down and skinned her knee, her mother would hold her and kiss her and tell her everything was going to be all right.

Being sick or injured was the only way to get people to notice her. Now she's in her sixties and she's still getting attention in the same old way.

It's not that Martha enjoys being sick. She doesn't at all. Nor is it true that all of her problems are in her head. Because she gets the attention she craves when she is having physical problems, her body may be predisposed toward illness. She would be the last one to believe that her life-style requires illness on her part, or that she consistently makes choices that detract from her well-being. But it is true that her desire for attention vastly outweighs her need to be healthy.

This is another example of the way a life-style can affect a person's life. The life-style is a consistent framework within which a person operates, even though he may not—in fact, probably does not—realize it.

As Dr. Rudolf Dreikurs put it:

> The individual may be convinced that he does not want what he brings about, but then he is merely not aware of the objectives he sets for himself. It is more difficult to recognize his basic goals which are the foundation of his lifestyle. . . . They represent a scheme of action by which the individual hopes to find his place in society. A set of convictions about himself and life which underlie his social movements.[3]

Once again, I have to use caution. Am I saying that all people who are chronically ill are victims of their life-styles? No, not at all, and I would never make such a general statement. But one must realize that a negative life-style can be a contributing factor to all sorts of problems—physical, emotional, and spiritual.

As a graduate student, I learned about the life-style as a theory put forward by Swiss psychologist Alfred Adler. At that time, I found it to be an intriguing and highly plausible theory to explain a great variety of human behavior. Since then, I've seen and heard the concept of life-style verified in hundreds, actually thousands, of cases.

For instance, I remember Leigh-Ann, a lovely young woman who couldn't understand why she kept falling in love with married men.

It wasn't intentional, she assured me. It was just one of those things that happened. Could she help it if all the best men were already taken? Or was it her fault if married men found her irresistible and single men didn't seem to notice her at all?

Leigh-Ann wasn't flippant or casual about her affairs with married men. She had an especially hard time dealing with the guilt because she was a born-again Christian, and she saw clearly that the situations she found herself in were not morally correct, even though she had literally dozens of excuses for her behavior.

I might never have met her if she had slipped once. But it happened a second time. And then a third. When relationships with four married men had come and gone within a space of three years, she decided to seek therapy—"Not because there's anything wrong with me, but I just thought maybe you could help me see why I keep letting these guys take advantage of me."

When I began looking into Leigh-Ann's background, I found an old familiar story. Her father had been a traveling salesman who was rarely home. He tried to express his love by showering her with "things," but he had generally been unable to verbally express his love for her, and she couldn't remember a single time he had hugged her or held her on his lap.

She resented my probing into her relationship with her father. She loved him, and he loved her, and any thought that their relationship wasn't exactly what it ought to be was preposterous!

I knew that Leigh-Ann really did love her father. And I also believed her when she told me that he loved her. After all, she was still getting the goodies to prove it.

If I mentioned her lovely new necklace, or expensive-looking jacket, or whatever else it might be, she would invariably say, "Oh, do you like this? My dad gave it to me."

Even though she was no longer a little girl, but a woman in her early thirties, her father was still trying to prove his love by giving her things instead of simply sitting down and spending some time with her, or calling her at the end of the day just to tell her he loved her. And even though she would never admit it to anyone, including herself, I could see that this was what she had really been missing all her life.

The truth was that over the years, her relationship with her father had built into her a life-style that said she was unworthy of a true, lasting love.

She wanted love. In fact she craved it. But at the same time she was afraid of it, and so she sought it out only in the "safety" of relationships with men who were already married, and who couldn't possibly expect more than a rendezvous in a motel or a clandestine meeting in an out-of-the-way restaurant.

And then she was in love again.

Guess what?

The guy was married. But this time it was different. He loved her more than anyone else had ever loved her before. They were drawn together like moths to a flame. It was fate. Think of every romantic cliché you've ever heard, mash them all up together, and these were the words she used to describe her relationship with this ethereal being who bore the strangely earthlike name of Richard.

But then one day the unthinkable happened. Richard left his wife and filed for divorce. He told Leigh-Ann that he and his wife hadn't been happy together anyway. Usually that's a tired and trite line for a married man who is on the prowl, but in this instance it happened to be true.

Leigh-Ann was, of course, ecstatic, because all of her dreams were about to become reality. But a funny thing happened on her way to happily-ever-after land.

Richard got his divorce all right. And as soon as he was a free man, he asked Leigh-Ann to marry him. But for some reason, all of a sudden *she wasn't so sure anymore.* (I bet you guessed this was coming three sentences ago.) She had once described Richard as her "knight in shining armor" (she was an intelligent woman, but she wasn't very original), but now there were more than a few rusty spots showing up on the boy's metallic suit.

She didn't know what to say to his marriage proposal, and I could only guess that Richard must have been devastated by her reluctance to commit to him. I knew from talking to Leigh-Ann that the couple had discussed marriage on many occasions. I was certain that Richard had never entertained any doubts about marrying Leigh-Ann. As far as he was concerned, all the romantic clichés she had used to describe their relationship were true, and they would watch the remaining years of their lives glide by in unending wedded bliss.

But Leigh-Ann's life-style, which led her to avoid commitment simply because she wasn't worthy, wasn't going to allow that to happen.

She kept Richard dangling for several months, until he eventually came to understand that she was never going to agree to marry him and walked away from the relationship. He wasn't used to being single, didn't like it, and so it didn't take him very long to find someone else. Within two or three months of his break with Leigh-Ann, he was engaged.

Can anyone tell me what happened next?

You guessed it.

Once Richard was engaged to another woman, Leigh-Ann suddenly rediscovered what a wonderful man he was, and how terribly wrong she'd been to let him get away. Her change of heart came too late, though, and Richard went ahead with his plans. At last report, he was happily married to the other woman.

He was wise enough to realize that Leigh-Ann only wanted what she couldn't have. Once something was in reach, it was suddenly not worth having anymore. Here again, her life-style dictated to her that real happiness should always be just out of her grasp.

Losing Richard was beneficial for Leigh-Ann in the long run, because it made her realize that she needed to change her attitude. She was willing, for the first time, really, to consider the fact that I might be right about her self-abusive tendencies. It wasn't so much that life was unfair to her as it was that she was unfair to herself, and sought out ways to deprive herself.

When Leigh-Ann came to realize that she had been inflicting damage on herself, she was taking a major first step toward changing things. Things didn't improve dramatically overnight. Her life-style was deeply ingrained into her personality. She still had that old tendency not to want anyone who wanted her.

It was like that old, tired joke:

"Welcome to the club, we're proud to have you as a member!"

"Are you kidding? I have too much pride to join any club that would even consider allowing the likes of me to be a member!"

Eventually, Leigh-Ann was able to free herself from that low opinion of herself. But it was really tough. She still slips back to her former thinking patterns sometimes. But she came to see her worth as a human being, and she was able, probably for the first time in her life, to enter into a strong give-and-take romantic relationship with an eligible bachelor.

Today, she is dating a fine man, and, because she loves him, doing everything within her power to strengthen and nurture the relationship. She is still single, but I would not be surprised if wedding bells are just around the corner.

Remember now, that Leigh-Ann's life-style was hidden well beneath the surface. If I had told you, upon your first meeting with her, that she had a very low opinion of herself and felt she was unworthy of a lasting love relationship, you might have wondered how many times I'd played football without a helmet.

She seemed to be self-assured, sophisticated, and intelligent, without a hint of an inferiority complex.

Yet lurking there, just beneath the surface of her bright, shiny exterior personality, was her true life-style, denying her the very thing she thought she wanted most in life—namely, a lasting relationship with a good man.

The life-style is not always hidden in that way. Sometimes it's fairly obvious.

Patricia, for instance, is a twenty-five-year-old graduate student who is also having trouble in the area of male-female relationships. Her problem is exactly the same as Leigh-Ann's, in that she only dates married men. But the reason for her behavior is closer to the surface.

Once again, it concerns her relationship with her father. In this situation, the father is extremely critical of his daughter. She has a hard time doing anything that pleases him and, in fact, has the feeling that she never has. At the same time, she is totally dependent upon him. He pays her tuition as a graduate student, buys her books, and gives her money to pay the rent and buy groceries.

She Takes the Cash *and* the Criticism

Daddy has always been generous with his money, but it comes with strings attached. Patricia has to put up with his complaining and criticizing. She has decided, perhaps unwisely, that it's a fair trade-off.

But her rather strained relationship with her father has colored the way she looks at men in general. Like any other woman (or man) she needs to be loved, and yet when it comes right down to it, she's afraid of men.

Patricia has never felt that her father would love her "no matter what," so her life-style demands that she only see men who would not have the opportunity to be disappointed with her.

In any long-term commitment, she feels as if she is ultimately doomed to failure. It's only a matter of time before she makes some terrible mistake and her lover discovers that she isn't really worthy of his passion.

So, to keep that from happening, she involves herself in short-term relationships with married men—one-night stands that couldn't possibly lead to anything more.

Patricia may not see it quite that way. She may think that she's just not ready for a lasting relationship. Wait until she gets her master's degree, and then maybe. . . . But unless she comes to see what she's doing, her doctorate will come next. Then her career. And so on.

The truth is that she's not too busy for a lasting relationship. She's just too frightened to look for one.

The difference between Leigh-Ann and Patricia is that Leigh-Ann has come to recognize the nature of her life-style and the hidden goals it brought to her existence. Patricia, up until now, still doesn't see her behavior for what it really is. And until she makes that breakthrough, she will be like the alcoholic who doesn't believe his drinking represents any real threat.

"I only drink because I want to drink," he says, "and I can quit anytime I want to!" Unfortunately, until he comes face to face with his problem, he'll never want to stop, and he'll go on through life destroying himself and those who love him.

As I said earlier, there are many varieties of life-styles, and, just to be sure that my examples of Leigh-Ann and Patricia don't leave the wrong impression, a life-style is not always reflected in the way a person behaves in "romantic" matters.

Robert, for instance, was a successful businessman who threw himself wholeheartedly into his work. He spent long hours at the job, seven days a week, and insisted, as many men do, that he was only doing it for the good of his wife and children.

Whenever his wife complained or told him she wished he'd spend more time with the children, that was his stock answer: "But I'm only doing it for you and the kids."

There was just enough truth in that statement to make her feel guilty about her "selfishness." He was a good provider, and she didn't mean to nag him about spending so many hours on the job.

But as the years went by, and the "goodies" began to pile up, Robert didn't show the slightest sign of slowing down. The woman in his life had all of the material possessions she could possibly want—and then some—but all of those things weren't enough to make up for the emptiness and loneliness in her life. She needed a man who would show his love for her by spending time with her, and she finally decided that she'd had enough.

She told her husband that unless he made a real effort to change his behavior, she wanted out of the marriage.

That's when he came to me.

It wasn't too hard to find out where Robert developed his workaholic life-style. When I asked him to tell me about his father, his reply was, "Oh, he was a good man. He was a hard worker." His favorite uncle? "Oh, that man really worked hard."

His mother was a hard worker, so were his brothers and sisters. In fact, every significant person in his life was described as a hard worker. He might tell me about his brother's athletic prowess, or his delightful sense of humor, but sooner or later, he'd get around to those magic words—"He was a hard worker."

The notion had been drummed into Robert's subconscious that a person's worth was determined by how hard he worked, and he was doing everything within his power to prove that he was a person of value. He had been so consumed with proving his self-worth that it almost cost him his family.

It took a while, but he was finally able to see that his long hours on the job had not been for his wife and children at all, but for himself. It wasn't easy for Robert to change his ways, but he did it.

At first he actually felt guilty spending a Saturday at the ball game with his kids, or using a Sunday afternoon for a picnic in the park. He was almost overcome by guilt on several occasions because he just "felt" that he ought to be at his office, taking care of business.

But to his credit, he didn't let his feelings control him. He successfully extricated himself from his workaholism and built new relationships with his wife and children. He was also surprised to discover that his business didn't suffer in the least because he began taking weekends off and working more reasonable hours during the week.

Now, lest anyone should misunderstand, please don't think that I'm against hard work. And I know there are times when husbands and wives have to spend more time on the job than they would really like to. That's especially true when someone has gone into business for himself and is trying to get things on a solid footing, or when the boss has given a rush job or a special project to one of his employees. But anyone who continues, week after week, month after month, year after year, to see most of his time taken up by his work ought to stop, step back, and assess his motives.

I could go on for hours about the development of the life-style, but the important thing is to understand that your life-style is a major reason for the things you do and the things that seem to "happen" to you.

The life-style in and of itself is neither negative or positive. It just is.

But if your life is a continuing cycle of frustration and rejection, your life-style is in need of repair. And it can be repaired.

Or if you're a parent of young children, you need to know how to help them develop a healthy life-style.

Too many people are living in a nightmare, when life was meant to be a dream!

3

How the Pattern Begins

The Early Years

What comes to your mind when you think about your childhood?

Happy hours, playing games with your friends, a house full of warmth and laughter?

Or do visions of failures come to mind—of not being able to do anything right, of your parents and teachers always angry with you because you'd let them down?

And, then, when you take a look into the future, what do you see? What sort of childhood will your own children remember? Will they look back fondly on a collection of happy memories, or will they see nothing but reasons to be glad those days are over?

If, when you look back, you see those unhappy events when you felt unworthy and rejected, it's primarily because someone in your life stressed your failures, overemphasized them, and magnified their importance to you. What happens to someone in the first seven years of his life—and especially the first four years—will shape the way he spends the rest of his life.

One of my clients, for instance, had a great deal of trouble building a healthy sex life with her husband. She told me that she loved him very much, and she wanted to enjoy being intimate with him, but she couldn't get it out of her head that sexual intercourse was repulsive and dirty.

Why? Because when she as three years old, her mother caught her "playing doctor" with the neighbor's four-year-old son. Actually, all they had been doing was giving in to a natural curiosity about the differences between the sexes. But Mary's mother had reacted as if she had just discovered that her daughter was personally responsible for starting World War II. Poor little Mary had been subjected to a severe tongue-lashing, the neighbor's boy had been chased out of the house, and the next thing she knew Mary found herself in the bathtub taking a hot bath, as if she had done something that made her dirty.

Even as she was approaching forty years of age, Mary still remembered how angry and ashamed her mother had been.

"I'll never forget the look on her face," she told me, "and how she kept telling me she was ashamed of me."

Mary's mother would have behaved much more wisely, of course, if she had been able to deal calmly with Mary and explain to her that, yes, there are differences between little boys and little girls, and that this is the way God made us. But, unfortunately for Mary, that's not what she did, and her daughter grew up fighting against her own sexual nature and viewing sex as something evil instead of good.

My point in bringing up Mary isn't to talk about how parents should tell their children about sex, but rather to point out how parental behavior can and does impact on children . . . far more than most of us realize.

A friend named Veronica was told by her doctor four years ago that she has multiple sclerosis. Naturally, the news was hard to take. She felt devastated and wondered how in the world this could happen to her, a young mother with two children under five years of age.

Ultimately, though, she made the decision to face this disease the way she had always faced troubles in her life. It was one more obstacle to be overcome. She wasn't going to give in to it, and she resolved that she would be the best wife and mother she could be, multiple sclerosis or no multiple sclerosis.

Today she's optimistic, always seems to be up, and except for her particularly bad days, you'd never know that she has the disease. It may not stay this way. Veronica is not ignorant about the effects of multiple sclerosis, and she knows that her future isn't all sunshine and blue skies. But she's determined to live every moment to the fullest and fight to live a normal life for as long as she can.

I admire her for her attitude. I also admire her family, her parents in particular, because I know the sort of people they are. They helped their daughter grow into a strong, can-do woman who is not about to let multiple sclerosis or anything else hold her back. The way Veronica has faced this dreadful disease is symbolic of her attitude—an attitude that was built into her personality during the first few years of her life. Her life-style has helped to provide her with the inner strength and character she needs now.

You may know someone like Veronica. In fact, you may even *be* someone like Veronica. But chances are you also know someone else whose life-style caused him to react to similarly bad news in a quite different way. Perhaps the minute the doctor told him there was something wrong, he crawled into bed and stayed there, already giving up hope. The person who reacts in that way is someone whose life-style is built on the premise that he can never measure up, that he is not good enough, and that he might as well get used to rejection and failure because that's all he's going to get in his life.

What a pity that some people are so afraid of life, and so incapable of overcoming tragedy when it strikes.

Now parents aren't totally responsible for the development of a child's life-style. There are many other people who enter into the life of that child and leave their mark—brothers and sisters, aunts and uncles, teachers, clergy, Sunday school teachers, coaches, scout leaders, and so on. But parents can and should take the leadership role in seeing to it that their children develop a healthy self-esteem and a positive life-style. Nobody else will have more impact on your child than you, and you should see to it that your involvement in his life brings a positive, constructive influence. If you are living a life of discouragement and rejection, chances are good that your parents have a lot to do with it. And, by the same token, you must do your best to see that the cycle doesn't repeat itself with your children, as it usually does.

What does it take to instill into your children a positive, can-do lifestyle? It takes patience, encouragement, giving of your time and energy, and something I call reality discipline. Let's talk about these qualities one at a time.

First consider patience.

What do you do when three-year-old Tommy spills his milk. One mom might react something like this:

"There you go again! I can't believe it! We can't have a single meal without your spilling your milk all over the place! All I ever do is clean up after you—and look—now there's milk all over the carpet."

If Mom is particularly angry she might even say something like, "You little inconsiderate slob! You've got to be the messiest boy I've ever seen in my life!"

Mom might feel a little bit better after letting off some steam, but her outburst certainly hasn't done her son any good. What's more, he believes what his mother says. If she says he's the messiest boy she's ever seen, it simply must be true. He knows he didn't mean to spill his milk, but there must be something wrong with him. He simply can't help it.

It's even worse for little Tommy if he has an older sibling who never spills his milk.

"I don't understand," Mom says, "why you can't be more like little Hurkimer over here? He never, ever makes a mess!"

There sits Hurkimer with a smirk on his face—a smirk that says, in essence, "I'm better than you. You're a little jerk who spills his milk, but I'm neat, and that makes me a better person." It also tells Tommy that his mother loves his older brother more than she loves him.

What would have been a proper response from Mom when her son spilled his milk?

"Woops, there goes the milk. Honey, can you get the rag and help me clean it up."

Okay, maybe that does sound a little bit like Supermom. And if, when Mom is in the middle of trying to take care of five things at once, Tommy pours a full glass of milk on her brand-new carpeting, her initial response isn't likely to be that gentle. So what's a harried mother or father to do.

Have you ever heard the old advice about counting to ten before reacting? Perhaps it sounds kind of trite, but it works.

I've also heard it said this way, "Be sure your brain is in gear before putting your mouth in motion."

You've probably seen those words before and possibly smiled to yourself as you read them. They are sort of comical, but they are also very true, especially when you're dealing with young children.

All children require patience, patience, and more patience.

In talking about Tommy and his spilled milk, I've hit upon another mistake that parents often make—usually without even realizing it.

"Look, honey," Dad says, when Tommy turns a somersault across the floor. "Remember when Louise first started doing that?"

"I sure do," his wife replies.

What does that tell Tommy? Well it tells him, first of all, that he hasn't done anything unique. Here the poor child has been practicing somersaults for two weeks, and he's so proud of himself for finally learning how to do them right. But when he proudly shows his parent what he's learned, they quickly deflate his ego by telling him they've seen this all before.

Mom and Dad don't realize that they've said anything wrong. They couldn't help but be reminded of how their daughter had done the same thing.

But parents need to understand that comparisons between children are never healthy. Comparisons with others always tell the child that he is not a unique individual, and that he is standing in someone else's shadow. Now my wife, Sande, and I have five children, so believe me, I know what you're talking about when you tell me that it isn't always easy to avoid comparisons. But what parents have to understand—and again, I'm speaking from personal experience—is that no two children are alike. They are individual human beings with individual strengths and weaknesses and must be treated as such.

The Case of Marvin the Frog

Let's say you have four children, the eldest three of which would have been right at home on the old "Father Knows Best" television show. That's to say they're good students, model citizens, and never give you any reason to have your blood pressure checked. And then there's little Marvin.

To say Marvin is different from the other three is like saying that Motley Crue's music is a bit different from that of Lawrence Welk.

On the first day of school, the teacher sends him home with a note that he was making strange noises in class.

So you ask him, "Marvin, dear, exactly what sort of strange noises were you making in class today?"

He looks at you with that mischievous smile and says, "I was pretending like I was a frog."

Well, how do you react to that?

"Listen, Marvin," you tell him, "I don't understand why you thought it was necessary to act like a frog and disrupt the class. Your older sisters, Marie and Margaret, never made noises like frogs in class. Neither did your brother Mark. They never gave us this kind of trouble, so why are you doing it?"

Now it is true that Marvin's mother and father need to speak to him about his behavior in class and take steps to see that it doesn't happen again. But they ought to try to do that without comparing him with his sisters and brother. The fact that they never acted like a frog in class doesn't really have anything to do with the fact that he did, and they ought to be left out of the situation.

What happens to Marvin if he comes home from school with a D in arithmetic, and he's the first one in the family to ever get a grade below C in anything? Dad says, "Marvin, I just don't know what's wrong with you. We've never had anyone come home with a D before!"

You see what sort of message Marvin is getting? That he's different, that he's not as good as his siblings, and that his parents are keenly disappointed in him.

I can already hear someone asking, "Well, if Marvin's misbehaving in class and just about to fail arithmetic, his parents really have to do something, don't they?" Certainly, but that's not the point! The point is that Marvin isn't Marie, Margaret, or Mark. He shouldn't be expected to act like them, and he shouldn't be compared with them.

I ought to mention, in case anyone misunderstands me, that avoiding comparisons does not mean that you ignore the individual strengths of your children. I believe that each person is born with certain abilities—gifts, if you prefer—that must be developed and encouraged. But to encourage one child in his particular skill does not require comparing him with others.

In the case of Marvin the frog, his teacher at school is well equipped to deal with Marvin and any other little croakers who are looking for extra attention. The teacher can clarify that she will not tolerate his disruption of the class, and if it continues, he will be disciplined. Saying anything more than that is saying more than is necessary.

I know it's hard—especially if you've got a wonderful good example sitting right there within arm's length—but don't use it. It takes patience to treat your children as individuals and to avoid comparing them with one another, but it's well worth the effort in the long run.

So be patient with your children, count to ten before saying anything you might regret, and discipline them with love. If you do that, you will not only be turning some of their defeats into victories, but you'll be teaching them lessons that will last a lifetime.

In addition to your patience, your children also need encouragement. In fact, encouragement and patience go hand in hand. But before I talk about what encouragement is, let me tell you what it's not.

First of all, it's not pushing your children beyond their ability to handle stress, trying to teach them to do higher mathematics by the time they're five years old. And it's not pushing little boys into sports programs where they're expected to behave like seasoned professionals. It's not tying your love and acceptance to your child's performance. I'm afraid that today's society has gone overboard when it comes to wanting our children to excel. There's nothing wrong with wanting the best for your children, but from what I've seen, I'm convinced that too many parents are using their children to show off in front of their peers.

"My Johnny is learning algebra and he's seven."

"Oh, yes, well, Juliekins speaks three languages fluently and she's six."

"That is wonderful. Of course, you know that my Calvin has just become the first-round draft choice of the New England Patriots and has his pre-acceptance into Harvard, and he's five and a half."

Okay, so I'm exaggerating. But not by much.

We have parents who are putting mobiles with advanced mathematic formulas into their children's cribs and reading to their two-year-olds from Plato and Cervantes. It's ridiculous, and what's more I haven't seen a single shred of credible evidence that it works.

What has this sort of pushing done for our society? It's given us stressed-out kids who have been robbed of their childhoods, that's what. We have a soaring suicide rate among teenagers, and it's no wonder.

Dr. R. Dean Coddington has published scales showing how many "stress points" certain events have in the lives of adolescents and children.[1] We've all seen the charts showing how stress piles up in the lives of adults, but we often make the mistake of thinking that the childhood years are happy-go-lucky and trouble free. They aren't. Dr. Coddington's charts show the results of selected events on the lives of our children:

Life Events Scale for Adolescents

The death of a parent	108
The death of a brother or sister	88
Divorce of your parents	70
Marital separation of your parents	62
The death of a grandparent	52
Hospitalization of a parent	52
Remarriage of a parent	51
Birth of a brother or sister	50
Hospitalization of a brother or sister	49
Loss of a job by your father or mother	46
Major increase in your parents' income	41
Major decrease in your parents' income	43
Start of a new problem between your parents	41
End of a problem between your parents	30
Mother beginning to work outside the home	28
Going on your first date	42
Breaking up with a boyfriend/girlfriend	39
Beginning the first year of high school	19
Moving to a new school district	41
Failing a grade in school	47
Getting your first driver's license	32
Being rewarded for a personal achievement	39

Being accepted into a college	39
Getting a summer job	35
Failing to achieve something you wanted	32
Deciding to leave home	41

Life Events Scale for Children

The death of a parent	109
The death of a brother or sister	86
Divorce of your parents	73
Marital separation of your parents	66
The death of a grandparent	56
Hospitalization of a parent	52
Remarriage of a parent	53
Birth of a brother or sister	50
Hospitalization of a brother or sister	47
Loss of a job by your father or mother	37
Major increase in your parents' income	28
Major decrease in your parents' income	29
Start of a new problem between your parents	44
End of a problem between your parents	27
Mother going to work outside the home	40
Beginning the first grade	20
Moving to a new school district	35
Failing a grade in school	45
Death of a pet	40
Being hospitalized for illness or injury	53
Finding an adult who really respects you	20
Getting an award for special achievement	34

I remember when I was an assistant dean of students at the University of Arizona and one of the students took his own life. John was a young man who had never received a grade lower than an *A* during four years of college, and who was about to be graduated summa cum laude. Yet he left a suicide note that said, "I just couldn't measure up to the standards of this world, perhaps in the next world I can do better."

How sad that a young man of such skill and intelligence, with his entire life ahead of him, should feel that he couldn't measure up. But that's what our society had taught him, and that's why we're seeing so many others who, like John was, are defeated perfectionists.

If parents aren't pushing their kids to excel academically, they push them in other areas, such as sports.

Now, don't get me wrong about sports. I love sports. I currently coach a junior high school girls' basketball team, and I've been involved in one sport or another for most of my life. I am proud to say that two young men I've coached in baseball have gone on to play in the big leagues. Sports can be a wonderful character builder, teaching teamwork, perseverance, and how to win—and lose—gracefully.

But far too many sports programs stress winning at all costs, and I'm appalled by much of what I see. Parents and coaches push small boys and girls beyond their abilities. Those with natural talent are singled out and turned into "stars," while those who aren't quite so gifted remain on the bench.

If Johnny hits a home run or scores a touchdown, he's his father's little man. But let him fumble the ball or strike out, and it's a totally different story. The simple fact is that if Johnny is doing his best, he ought to be congratulated for his efforts, regardless of the outcome of those efforts.

Encourage him when he does exceptionally well, yes, but don't hold it against him when he doesn't. And make sure that he knows that your love and acceptance of him is constant, no matter how well he performs on the ball field.

In short, have the patience to let your children be who they are. Don't try to force them to be what you always wanted them to be, and don't be exasperated with them if they fail once in while.

I'll never forget an incident that happened to me when I was twelve years old and playing Little League baseball in upstate New York. At the conclusion of the season, I was proud and excited to be named as the starting third baseman for my league's all-star team. Now every Little League in the country fields an all-star team, and a worldwide single elimination tournament gets underway, with the eventual championship to be decided at the Little League World Series in Williamsport, Pennsylvania. Every Little Leaguer dreams of making it to Williamsport.

Well, our team won its first two games of all-star competition, but we found ourselves locked in a real battle in the third one. Going into the bottom of the sixth (and final) inning, the score was tied at 2–2. Our manager had made some changes in the lineup trying to get a run across in an earlier inning, so I found myself playing first base—an unfamiliar position.

The opposing team opened the inning with a single. This was followed by two quick outs, which allowed the runner to advance to third base.

We were in a spot of trouble, but all we needed was one more out and the game would go into extra innings.

Here came the pitch, the batter swung, and it was a soft grounder up the middle of the infield. The shortstop easily scooped up the ball and fired a perfect strike in my direction.

I stretched out to take the throw . . . the ball was in my glove . . . and then it popped out. I grabbed for it again, but couldn't get it. It was too late. I had dropped the ball, the winning run had scored, the game, and the season, was over.

I couldn't believe what I had done. There were no excuses. The sun hadn't been in my eyes. It hadn't been a bad throw. The runner hadn't bumped into me. I had, pure and simple, dropped the ball.

To say I was upset and disappointed doesn't begin to describe the way I felt. If I could have, I would have melted into first base. Tears filled my eyes, and I felt totally deflated. How could I go back to the dugout and face my teammates, knowing that I had let them down—that my mistake had cost them their dreams.

Fortunately for me, our manager was a wise man who knew exactly how I felt.

He came out of the dugout to meet me as I made my way back across the infield. Before I could say anything, he had his arm around me.

"Listen, Kevin," he said, "if it hadn't been for you, we never would have made it this far, and I want you to remember that. You've been doing a good job all year, so keep your head up."

How thankful I was, and still am, that he understood. His encouraging words went a long way toward helping me deal with the situation. No, I didn't immediately forget about what I had done or shrug it off. But today, quite a few years later, I look back upon my days in Little League as a time of great happiness and fun.

What would have happened if the manager hadn't been so supportive, if he had berated me and let me know in no uncertain terms that I had let everyone down?

You know, I didn't need anyone to tell me I had made a mistake. I already knew that. If he, or anyone else, had reinforced that, it would have crushed me.

If the subject of Little League came up I might say, "I don't want to talk about Little League. I'll never forget how I dropped a throw in a very important game and cost my team a victory!" But I'm thankful that I was playing for a man who didn't think less of me as a person simply because I dropped an easy throw. He separated my action from my worth as a human being, and that's something all parents must strive to do.

I'm sure that as long as I live I'll never forget dropping that ball. But neither will I ever forget the encouragement given to me by a man who knew that a young boy's feelings mattered more than winning a baseball game.

The Christian Church talks about separating the sin from the sinner, or hating the sin but loving the sinner. I'd say that's very good advice, especially for parents who don't want their children growing up to be defeated perfectionists.

What do I mean by separating the sin from the sinner?

Well, suppose that at the end of a hard day you go into your daughter's room to discover that she has been lying on the floor using her finger paints, with the result that paint has spilled on the carpet in several places. What's more, you have a very strict rule that finger paints are to be used only at the dining room table.

A typical response might be something like, "Joanne! What in the world do you think you're doing! I've told you and told you and told you that you're not supposed to paint in your room, but as usual, you just ignore me. You are so irresponsible, and you make me so angry . . . I just don't know what I'm going to do with you! I don't know if you're not listening to me when I tell you things, or if you're just dumb!"

How does little Joanne respond to this? By thinking, *Mom's right. I never listen to her and I never do anything right. I'm a bad girl, I'm stupid, and now she hates me!*

But, if Mom had been able to separate the sin from the sinner, or the act from the actor, she would have simply addressed the problem.

"Joanne, you know you're not supposed to paint in your bedroom. See, you've gotten paint on the carpet, and that's exactly why you're not allowed to paint in here. Because you've disobeyed me, I am going to take your paints, and you won't be allowed to use them for a week."

This response doesn't let Joanne off the hook. She still knows she's done something wrong, and that she will have to suffer the consequences of her actions. But it doesn't damage her self-esteem, and it doesn't make her feel that her mother is rejecting her. Sure, she may complain about having her paints taken away, or ask her mother for another chance, but deep down she knows that she has done wrong and respects Mom's decision to take her paints away for a time.

Mom Loves Me . . . If I'm Good!

Now there's another side to this coin of keeping the act and the actor separated, and that's the mistake parents make of teaching their children that they love them only when they're good. This is called conditional love, and parents who practice it are producing within their children the belief that "I'm loved only when I behave myself, or when I get good grades," or whatever else it might be that Mom and Dad tie their love and approval to.

As an example of conditional love, say Dad is out in the yard raking leaves. Five-year-old Jessica wants to help, so she grabs an extra rake out of the garage and pitches in.

Her admiring and appreciative dad smiles at her and says, "Thank you, honey. I love you for helping me!"

Now, on first glance, it's hard to see that Dad has done anything wrong. After all, the only thing he wanted to do was tell his little girl that he appreciated her help and that he loves her. But the problem comes because he has tied his love for her to the fact that she is helping him.

Jessica thinks happily to herself, *Daddy loves me because I'm helping him.* I know that someone is bound to ask, "You mean one little incident like that is going to hurt a child's self-esteem?"

The answer is no, probably not. But problems do arise when this sort of response is repeated:

"I love you, Bobby, because you keep your room so neat and clean!" "You got three *As*? My, what a good girl! I love you!" "Thank you for setting the table, Donna. I love you when you help me like this."

When your children misbehave they must be disciplined, and, conversely, when they go out of their way to do something nice for you, they need to be thanked and told that their efforts are appreciated. But through it all, whether they're being disciplined or being thanked, they need to know that Mom and Dad love them, and that that love has nothing to do with the child's "performance." A child who grows up thinking that he must always strive to "earn" his parents' love will not have a well-developed sense of his innate worth.

So encouragement is not pushing your children beyond their abilities, and it is not basing your approval of them on their performance. I'll tell you another thing it isn't, and that's praise. If you want to praise someone, praise God, but don't praise your children. When you do, it rings hollow, and it doesn't produce self-esteem and confidence in them.

Encouragement comes when you center on your child's efforts, telling him that he has done well, that he has improved, or that you are pleased with the progress he has made. Praise differs from this in that it centers, once again, on the child's worthiness.

If Bobby has surprised you by thoroughly cleaning his room, an encouraging response would be, "Your room really looks nice. You did a great job! Thank you!"

A praising response would be, "You cleaned your room. Here's five dollars. What a good boy you are!"

The difference between the two responses is slight, but there is a vast difference between the messages received. Praising suggests that your approval of your child is based on his performance. For that reason, I suggest that parents avoid saying things like, "I'm so proud of you! Your trumpet solo was beautiful." Go ahead and tell your child that he played beautifully, but it is best to leave off the part about being proud of him because of it.

In my book *Parenthood Without Hassles—Well Almost*, I included the Child's Ten Commandments. Commandment number six says, "I need your encouragement, but not your praise, to grow. Please go easy on the criticism; remember, you can criticize *the things I do* without criticizing *me*."

Admittedly, some psychologists would argue with me about the difference between praise and encouragement, or say I'm quibbling over semantics. But my years of counseling experience tell me otherwise. Encouragement is aimed at creating growth in your children, whereas praise can actually stifle your child's growth and help make him into a defeated perfectionist who thinks that he is not worthy of love and respect unless he does things exceptionally well.

One way you can really encourage your child is by standing back and letting him do things on his own. Far too many parents think they have to do everything for their children. This, too, is a form of rejection, although many parents have trouble believing this.

Let's say that you're an absolute nut about the way a bed should be made. If it's not made just right, with the pillows fluffed up just so, and the corners of the bed spread exactly square, the whole room looks like a mess to you.

And then one morning little Melinda calls you into her room.

"Look, Mommy," she says proudly, pointing at what looks to you like something a wrestling match has just taken place on, "I made my bed."

Fighting back your first impulse, whether to scream or faint, you say, "Honey, that's great!"

Later on, as soon as Melinda is safely outside, you sneak into her room and remake her bed, exactly the way you like it.

Nothing else is ever said about it, and so you figure that Melinda doesn't know what you did. But she does. And she knows that her effort wasn't good enough. She feels rejected.

What should you have done? You should have fought off your understandable impulses to fix the bed up the way you wanted it, and left it the way Melinda had made it.

There is a time for training, to take Melinda aside and show her the correct way to make her bed, but you can do that at another time so that it doesn't take away from her sense of accomplishment. You don't have to lie to her and tell her that hers is the best-looking bed you've ever seen, but you can thank her for making it, tell her you appreciate it, and let it go at that.

By remaking the bed for her you're not only rejecting her, but you're sending a message that, "It really doesn't matter what I do, because Mommy is going to do it over again." If you feel inclined to walk around behind your children, doing again what they've already done, you're hurting them and yourself. You shouldn't have to spend your life as the policeman of your family, following everybody around and correcting the mistakes they've made.

And Dad, if you can't understand why I'm going on for so long about making a bed, to help you understand, let's say that after she's made her bed, Melinda helps you wash the car. She is so proud of being able to be a helper for Daddy, but then she sees you going back over the area she's already washed.

"Daddy," she says, "I already cleaned that part."

What should you do? If she missed a few spots, let them stay dirty. Your child's sense of accomplishment and self-esteem is worth much more than a clean car or a well-made bed any day.

Am I saying that Melinda should still be allowed to get away with a sloppily made bed when she's eleven? Of course not. By that time, she should know how to make her bed properly.

Motive is important here, just as it is everywhere else. If your son just mowed the lawn for the first time, and he missed a few places here and there, you can chalk it up to his inexperience and figure that he will improve each time he does it. But if he's sixteen years old and he did a haphazard job because he was anxious to go off with his friends, he should be held accountable. I'll talk more about that later, when I touch upon the concept of reality discipline. But for now, the point I want to make is that your children will not be encouraged, but discouraged, if you show them through your words or actions that their efforts were not good enough for you.

Another bit of good advice, if you want to encourage your children and help them avoid falling into the cycle of self-condemnation and rejection, is to focus on the positive instead of the negative.

What do I mean by that? Let's say Melinda is a little bit older now, and she comes to tell you that she's cleaned her room and she wants you to see it. When you walk into it, you see that she has, indeed, done a good job of straightening up the room.

Except for one minor detail. For some reason, she seems to have overlooked her jacket, which lies sprawled across her dresser, instead of hanging in the closet where it ought to be.

What do you say?

Probably something like this:

"Well, honey, you did a terrific job—but you forgot to hang up your jacket."

Melinda's proud smile quickly disappears.

"I knew you wouldn't like it," she whines.

"Honey, I like it . . . in fact I love it. It's just that you forgot to hang up your jacket."

By this time, there's not much you can do to rectify the situation. Melinda feels hurt and rejected, and no amount of backtracking on your part is going to make her feel better. *What's the use of ever trying,* she thinks. *I can't do anything to please Mom and Dad.*

Am I saying that Melinda should be allowed to leave her jacket laying around anywhere she wants to? Of course not. But I am saying that there is a time for overlooking the negative and focusing on the positive.

Believe it or not, all children want to please their parents—to have Mom and Dad be proud of them. And nothing hurts a child as much as doing something he's very proud of, only to have his parents find fault with it. If you want to turn your child into a defeated perfectionist, that's a very good place to begin. There was a popular song quite a few years ago which advised people to "accentuate the positive," and I'd have to say that's still good advice, especially when dealing with children.

Overprotection Equals Rejection

The idea of letting children do things on their own refers to more than just cleaning rooms and making beds, too.

I have counseled many men and women who have been held back in life because of overprotective parents. It's a special problem for men whose mothers had a hard time letting go.

Overprotection is not really loving and helpful. Instead, it's a form of rejection. The child whose parents do everything for him comes to believe that he is incapable of doing anything for himself. His parents are undoubtedly acting out of the purest motives, but the message he gets is, "They have to do all this for me because they know I'm too stupid to do it for myself."

Then, he finds himself grown, on his own, and he doesn't have anyone to take care of him anymore. He's resentful because he doesn't really know how to take care of himself. He's always had someone who would run interference for him. He knows he's incapable of success in life, and so his life fulfills his prophecy of failure.

If he ever does get married, it's probably going to be to someone who acts more like a parent than a partner and an equal. It won't be a healthy relationship.

If you really love him, Mom, let him fall on his face once in a while. Having to put up with a few bumps and scrapes along the way is much better than having to put up with a lifetime of failure and rejection.

Giving your child the chance to fail is another way of encouraging him.

It's the wise parent, too, who is aware of subtle ways children are being rejected, and who acts to correct the situation.

I remember one situation where a couple had twin boys named Ricky and Robby. The only difference in their appearance was that Robby had brown hair and his brother had a crop of flaming red hair that set him apart in any crowd. Whenever people met the boys for the first time, you can guess what they would say:

"My, what beautiful red hair!"

"Where in the world did you get that hair?"

All the attention was showered on the little redhead, while his brother stood by silently, wanting to shout, "I'm here, too!"

In this case, it wasn't the parents making unfavorable comparisons, but well-meaning friends and strangers. Nobody would have hurt Robby's feelings on purpose; they just didn't understand that their constant fussing over Ricky was tantamount to telling Robby that *he* was dull and boring.

At first, the parents didn't realize what effect this was having on Robby. But when the boy began to misbehave and defy their authority, they were perceptive enough to realize he was making a bid for their attention.

They began to look for special ways to encourage him, to make him understand that he was every bit as important as his brother. And, when total strangers would come up to them in restaurants or shopping malls and begin cooing about Ricky's gorgeous hair, they would make a point of introducing Robby and seeing to it that he was not left out of the conversation.

Once Robby came to see that he was not going to be confined to life in his brother's shadow, his behavior improved immensely. After a while he wasn't even jealous of his brother's hair anymore.

Meanwhile, it is unfortunate but true that our society places far too much emphasis on appearance. This is true of society at large, which worships men and women with perfect faces and bodies, and it's also true of parents. Parents will tend to favor their better-looking children.

One friend confided to me that he had had a particularly rough time going through life as one of the Newman Brothers.

"What do you mean, Newman Brothers?" I asked him. "Your last name is Snodgrass."

"I consider us the Newman Brothers," he said, "because my brother looks like Paul, and I look like Alfred E."

At least he was able to joke about it. But I knew that he really didn't think it was funny. And I'll tell you something else, too. The guy did not look anything like Alfred E. Neuman. But because his older brother had been so much better looking when they were young and had teased him constantly about his appearance, he had come to view himself as extremely unattractive.

He let his embarrassment over his appearance hold him back in several ways. He had not dated much, he had not pursued topnotch jobs, all because he believed that people found him unattractive. What woman would want to go out with him? What organization would want him to represent them? And so on.

It didn't matter what he saw when he looked in the mirror or saw photographs of himself. He was convinced that he was ugly, and there was nothing anyone could do to talk him out of it. Without the intervention of professional help, he was destined to live a discouraged, defeated life.

Well, we might as well face up to the truth. The Declaration of Independence is wrong when it says that everyone is created equal. It's just not true. Especially lookswise.

Children who aren't exceptionally attractive are especially in need of encouragement and love. The last thing in the world they need is to be teased about their looks. If Patsy's eyes are crossed and she has protruding ears, she doesn't need anyone to tell her that she's no Angelina Jolie. She knows that already.

Sure, she may act as if she thinks it's funny and laugh when her brother teases her, but inside she's dying.

I knew of one case where a man was angry when his wife became pregnant. The couple were in their late thirties, already had three children, and he wasn't interested in having another one.

He probably would have pushed his wife to have an abortion, but because he was a Christian he decided to do the "spiritual" thing and just treat his wife and unborn child as if they were rubbish. (As if the whole thing were their fault.)

To add to this poor child's misfortune—well, let me put it this way: When the baby was in the nursery at the hospital, nobody ever tapped on the window and said, "Oh, look at that cute little boy over there."

No, the Johnsons had three fine-looking children, and now a new addition to the family who just wasn't in the same league, lookswise.

You've heard the expression, "A face that only a mother could love." That was apparently the case here, because Mom was delighted with her tiny little boy, but Dad took one look at him and his heart grew harder.

As time went by, things didn't change. The other children were the lights of their father's life, but the youngest son could barely get the time of day from him. Because Mom was resentful of the way her baby was being treated, she began to favor him, pamper him, and overprotect him. That meant the poor kid was being rejected on two accounts. It also meant that the other children were resentful of their little brother—and so family life was anything but pleasant.

It was Mom who first decided she needed to seek out professional help. (I'm sorry, men, but women are usually much more perceptive about problems and more willing to seek help.)

She came to see that she needed to encourage her small son, who was then three years old, but not to smother him with her love. She also saw that it was not the fault of her older children that they were better looking than the baby, or that their father treated them better. They needed her loving encouragement, too, and shouldn't have to feel that Mom had shut them out of her life because of her special child.

Finally, she was able to find enough courage to tell her husband that she was sick and tired of his pettiness, that she wasn't going to tolerate it anymore, and that she expected some changes.

At first he was angry and sullen, getting involved in one of his "patented pouts."

But after a while, his wife's persistence broke through. He acknowledged that he "might have been" wrong in a few areas, and finally agreed that he, too, would come for counseling.

Admittedly, Mom was taking some risks when she gave her husband an ultimatum and told him that she wasn't going to put up with his childish behavior any longer. He might have said, "Fine with me," and walked out the door, but he didn't. In this case, Mom's course of action paid off. But even if it hadn't, Mom had to take the risk, for the sake of the entire family.

It's unfortunate that our society places so much emphasis on looks, but because it does, children who do not look like little fashion models must be made to understand that they are special people, every bit as worthy as anyone else. Otherwise, they may grow up to live the hard life of the defeated perfectionist.

The same is true of handicapped youngsters, whether their handicaps are physical or mental.

If you've spent time with groups of children, you know that they can be awfully cruel, and anyone who is the least bit different is going to be picked on.

The girl with thick glasses may be called "four-eyes," and the boy with the learning deficiency, "dummy" or "stupid." And then there are the boorish adults who will accost the parents of such children in public places and ask questions such as, "Oh dear, what's wrong with her eyes?" Or, "How come he's in the wheelchair?"

They always direct those "none-of-your-business" questions at the parents, talking right over the children as if they're not really there. That's a double form of rejection because it centers, first of all, on the child's handicap, and then it treats the child as if he's less than a person, incapable of understanding or answering a question for himself.

If you're the parents of a handicapped child, you have it especially hard, because it's difficult to know when you're doing too much for him. You know he needs special help in a number of areas, but you have to be careful that you don't overdo it.

Your goal should always be to see to it that he does everything he possibly can in spite of his handicap. At the same time, you must try to protect him from unnecessary rejection. As parents we're all up there on the tightrope, walking that fine line between not doing enough and doing too much—but for parents of handicapped children, that tightrope is even thinner and harder to walk.

Go Ahead and Be Rude

Suppose you were out with little Patsy, who is confined to a wheelchair, and someone walked up to you and said, "What's the matter with her?"

I'll tell you what I'd say: "Why don't you ask her? She can tell you—if she wants to."

Perhaps that's a bit rude, but no more so than the boor's original question. Besides that, it shows respect for Patsy, and reaffirms her worth as a person.

Now because I've done so much talking about letting your children do things on their own, and allowing them to get a few scrapes once in a while, you may have come to the conclusion that I'm opposed to picking your children up and comforting them when they fall.

That is not the case. Your children need to be held and comforted, but you can do that without making excuses for them or telling them they were right about something, when they weren't.

For instance, let's say your Julie, who is used to getting As and Bs in school, comes home with a C– in English. This is a big problem for her, and as she tells you about it she begins to cry. "It's all Mrs. Cranston's fault," she blubbers. "She just doesn't like me, and she won't give me a good grade no matter what I do."

But you happen to know that Mrs. Cranston is a good teacher who expects her students to put forth some effort in her class. And you also know that Julie hasn't been spending much time on her homework lately.

There are several ways you could respond. You might say, "Well, I'm sorry about that, honey. It's really tough when a teacher doesn't like you, but you just do the best you can." Or you might say, "Don't come crying to me with a C–. You ought to be ashamed of yourself."

Neither one of those responses is particularly helpful. In the first one, you're agreeing with the child that it's not really her fault, absolving her of all blame in the matter. In the second response, you're completely ignoring the child's feelings, overlooking the fact that she feels bad enough already about her grade. In that instance you're adding rejection on top of rejection.

A proper response would be something like this: "Honey, I'm sorry you feel so badly about the grade, but I'm sure it's not because Mrs. Cranston doesn't like you. You're just going to have to buckle down and do some hard work during the next nine weeks and prove to her you can get an *A* in her class."

You might also tell her that you're happy she wants to do well in school, but that one *C–* isn't the end of the world.

(Yes, I know parents who ground their children for bringing home *C*s, or, in one instance, even a *B*. These are parents who are adding their children to the ranks of defeated perfectionists—people who will never be satisfied with themselves because they can't attain that "perfect" state their parents demand of them.)

In my book, *Making Children Mind Without Losing Yours*, I discussed several steps involved in comforting children.[2] These are worth repeating here, because how you deal with your child's hurts and failures has a great bearing on whether or not he will become a discouraged and defeated adult.

The steps are:

1. Listen—to what the child is saying and, more importantly, what he is feeling.

2. Respond to the child's feelings. Let him know that you've heard him and you understand why he feels the way he does. "I understand how badly you feel about fumbling that ball." If the same kind of thing has ever happened to you, tell him about that, and let him know you felt the same way. It might not make him feel better instantly, but it will at least let him know that he's not the first one who's ever felt this way.

3. Touch. Never be afraid to reach out and touch your child, whether it's taking him on your lap when he's younger, hugging him, or just touching him on the shoulder. Touching is an important way to communicate your love and care for him.

As Dr. Ross Campbell says, "Remember that physical contact, especially the more affectionate type (holding, hugging, kissing, etc.) is vital to boys during their younger years. The younger the boy, the more vital affectional contact is to him. While with a girl, physical contact (especially the more affectionate type) increases in importance as she becomes older and reaches a zenith around the age of 11. Nothing stirs my heart more than an 11-year-old girl who is not receiving adequate emotional nourishment. What a critical age!"[3] A gentle touch can communicate so much love and caring, and that's important to remember.

4. Always look for alternatives. Suppose the family has been planning a trip to see the local baseball team in action. But when the big day comes, the skies open up in a downpour and the game is canceled. Telling your child, "Well, these things happen. They're just a part of life, so you'd better get used to them," doesn't help at all. Neither does becoming angry with him because he can't contain his disappointment. Ask him if there is anything else he would like to do. If not, suggest a few things. Perhaps the family can all go out to see a movie—or go to the child's favorite pizza parlor for dinner. He may not jump at any of your suggestions at first, because he's so disappointed about not seeing the baseball game. But after he's had a few moments to think about it, he'll come around and the family can have its fun day after all.

5. Give the child a choice. After examining all the alternatives, let him make the choice as to what he wants to do. If you make choices for him, you are being disrespectful and saying, in essence, "You're not capable of making a wise choice, so I'll have to do it for you."

6. Never accept excuses. If you do that, you're encouraging your child to keep the blame fixed on someone else. Julie claimed her *C–* in English came because her teacher didn't like her. That statement shifted the blame away from herself and onto Mrs. Cranston, and if Mom and Dad agree with her, Julie will never learn to face up to her own responsibilities.

7. See your child's mistakes not as defeats or frustrations, but as building blocks. Your child will learn from his mistakes and you can, too. It is always important to treat setbacks as positive lessons, as steps to improvement and learning so you can do better next time.

8. Encourage commitment. Don't take your child's problems upon your shoulders and solve them for him. Work with him, yes, but encourage him to persevere, and, if he can, to solve the problems through his own efforts.

9. Be ready to evaluate the problem. In other words, always be ready to give your support and encouragement. Don't let the child thrash around in confusion and bewilderment. If the way he has chosen to solve his problem isn't going to work, be prepared to step in and discuss another way of approaching things. If you see your child trying to solve a problem in a way that is really only going to make things worse, don't look the other way and think, *Well, I suppose this will be a good lesson for him.* Children sometimes make wrong choices, and when they do, they require some parental guidance and advice.

Do I mean that you, as a parent, should step into the situation at the last moment, like some sort of caped avenger, and set things right? No, that's not what I mean. You should still let your child work out the problem, but your job is to suggest alternative approaches and plans. And another thing is very important—don't become a Monday morning quarterback. Do you know what a Monday morning quarterback is? That's a fellow who has twenty-twenty hindsight. He can always tell you what you've done wrong, but it's always after the fact.

What I'm saying is that your children don't need anyone to come along after they've goofed something up and tell them in a critical sort of way what they *should* have done—especially when it's already obvious to them.

I tell my clients that they should never "should" on themselves or their children, looking back over past events and telling themselves what they *should* have done. This sort of Monday morning quarterbacking doesn't produce any beneficial results. All it does is reinforce the idea that "I never do anything right. Why do I even try?"

Suppose you were putting a new brand of fertilizer on your front lawn. You weren't sure of the setting, so you accidentally used too much, turning a large portion of your lawn a less-than-beautiful shade of brown.

A couple of days later, you're standing there surveying the damage, when along comes Helpful Hal, your know-it-all neighbor. "Boy," he says, "looks to me like you used too much fertilizer."

"Really?" you ask, in a tone that's supposed to convey sarcasm, only he doesn't pick up on it.

"Yeah, you should have measured it more carefully."

Now, let me ask you this: Is old Hal really being helpful?

Of course not. You already know that you used too much fertilizer, that you should have measured more carefully, and so on. All your neighbor's comments will do is make you even more angry.

If this kind of "help" has that effect on you, it will have the same effect on your child.

Suppose your teenage son comes in from a trip to his favorite hamburger place. You're sitting around talking, when a look of panic suddenly comes across his face.

"Oh, no!" he says, as he reaches into his hip pocket for his wallet.

"What's wrong?"

He opens his wallet, looks into it, and then shakes his head as if his worst fears have been confirmed.

"I just remembered. I gave the girl at the counter a twenty, but she only gave me enough change for a five."

What do you say?

"Son, you've got to be more careful. You should always remember to count your change," or, "Well, didn't you remember that you gave her a twenty?"

In response to that last question, he might say something like, "Yes, of course I remembered that I gave her a twenty, it's just that I love being shortchanged."

That's rather sarcastic and disrespectful, of course, but who could blame him. He knows he made a mistake. He also knows that, even if he runs right back to the hamburger place, chances of recovering his loss are slim. Your son has learned a powerful lesson through the loss of his money. He doesn't need that lesson reinforced by a parent who "shoulds" and nags him and, in essence, makes him feel like a failure.

As a matter of fact, nagging your children is never good for them, or you. It makes them resentful, and it also causes them to believe that you see them as irresponsible and unworthy of your trust. Eventually, they will begin to agree with you—to see themselves in the same way. Nagging serves to discourage rather than encourage.

So what do you do? I can hear the lament of every mother right now: "If I don't nag him he'll never do anything."

If I asked a hundred mothers selected at random how often they have to remind their teenage child, on an average day, to make his bed, I'd be willing to bet the answers would average somewhere between three and four.

How many times do you have to call your children to the table for dinner? My experience tells me that the average answer is three.

Why? It's because parents have come to believe they have to nag their children and the children, on the other hand, have come to expect being nagged. Until Mom's (or Dad's) voice has risen an octave or two and taken on a harder edge, there's no reason to pay a whole lot of attention.

One mother complained that she couldn't get her daughter to do anything when she was supposed to. Although she was nagged, threatened, and punished repeatedly, her room stayed a mess. Mom would say, "Laura, I want you to pick your clothes up off the floor before you go out to play."

"Okay, Mom."

Ten minutes later, Mom would hear the front door slam, a signal that Laura had run off to play with her friends. But what would Mom find in Laura's room? You guessed it. The clothes she had agreed to pick up still sprawled across the floor.

Laura wasn't openly rebellious. In fact, whenever Mom asked her to do something, she'd happily agree. But she never followed through.

Her excuse was always the same:

"I'm sorry, Mom. I just forgot."

"How could you forget? I asked you not more than ten minutes ago to pick these clothes up! Can't you remember to do anything I ask you to do?"

Day after day, week after week, it went like this, and the constant skirmishes between Laura and her mother threatened to break into an all-out war. Laura would always promise to do better next time and beg her mother not to punish her. When Mom wouldn't give in, Laura would retreat to her room, lock her door, and sulk. Both of them were resentful, and Laura was just about to work herself into the *Guinness Book of World Records* under "Most Times Grounded in a Single Year."

Laura's mother could see that she wasn't getting anywhere at all, and finally agreed that another approach was needed.

It was suggested that she and Laura work out a contract. Laura, in fact, was to be the one to write it out, with Mom's approval. After they had agreed upon the terms of the contract and signed their names to it, it would be affixed to the refrigerator door, where both could check it whenever they wanted to.

The contract spelled out what Laura's daily and weekly duties were, as well as what the punishment would be if she didn't keep her part of the agreement.

Laura's duties listed on the contract included doing her homework, seeing to it that her cat was fed each morning, setting the table for dinner each night, and so on. It was also agreed that Laura would clean her room every Saturday afternoon, and that Mom would be allowed to inspect and make sure it had been cleaned to her satisfaction. Mom agreed not to complain about the way the room looked the rest of the week.

The contract also stipulated that it wasn't Mom's job to remind Laura about any of the things she had to do. Nor, if Laura forgot to do something, was Mom allowed to alter the provisions of the contract with regard to punishment. This was to be viewed as an ironclad, binding contract that both parties must agree to live by. And, in fact, Laura was even encouraged to help decide what her discipline should be if she failed to perform any of her assigned duties.

Failure to clean her room, for instance, carried the punishment of going without television for a week. If Saturday came and went and the room hadn't been cleaned, watching television was out the window. Even if she remembered Saturday night, or Sunday afternoon, and cleaned her room in such a way that would have earned her a gold medal at the Olympic room cleaning competition—well, that was too bad because it wasn't living up to the provisions of the contract.

Laura's improvement began immediately after posting the contract, which seemed to work almost as well as a Jerry Lucas memory course. It was amazing how quickly Laura developed a better memory. And as for Mom, she was more relaxed and happy to have her nagging days behind her. After all, no woman enjoys being a nag.

Yes, there were still those occasions when Laura failed to live up to the provisions of the contract, and when she begged her mother to let her off the hook.

But Mom would say, "You know I can't do anything about it," and show Laura where, in her own handwriting, she had agreed what her consequence would be if she failed to perform up to the expected standards.

Once Laura realized that it wasn't really "mean old Mom" who was punishing her, her relationship with her mother improved.

Another thing happened, too—Laura began to see that she could remember things if she tried. She was learning to be a responsible citizen of her family. Prior to the contract, whenever she had failed to do what she was supposed to do, she would say things like, "Well, what do you expect? You know I'm stupid." Or, "I can't help it if I can't remember. I've never been very smart." Those sorts of comments had been self-fulfilling, too, as Laura really had begun to believe that she wasn't bright. Consequently, she wasn't doing as well in school. She just didn't think she could catch on to new concepts in math and English.

But it's been several months now since Laura has failed to clean her room by her Saturday deadline. And although there's been an occasional slipup on some of the smaller items, her overall record has been nothing less than spectacular.

She has been encouraged tremendously to discover that she does have a sharp mind, that she can remember things, and that she doesn't really need someone to stay on her back all the time. In short, she's come to see herself as responsible for her own actions, and that attitude has carried over into other areas of her life, such as in her schoolwork. What's more, the relationship between mom and daughter has improved to the point where it's better than it had been in years.

Most importantly, there's a harmonious, encouraging attitude within the family, and Laura's self-esteem has grown tremendously as a result of coming to understand that she can be capable and responsible.

And any child who grows up in an encouraging atmosphere is most likely going to grow into a positive, productive adult.

Don't Fall for the Big Lie

So far, we've seen that it takes patience, and encouragement, to build a healthy approach to life into your children. It also takes your willingness to give of your time and energy.

Now a lot of people today have fallen for a big lie when it comes to spending time with their children. Actually, they haven't fallen for it so much as jumped for it, because it excuses them from not living up to their responsibilities.

What is this big lie? It goes something like this: "It's not the quantity of time I spend with my children, it's the quality."

There's only one way to describe that kind of reasoning: "It's grade-A, 100-percent bullcrumble.

Any parent who thinks he can be with his child for a few minutes a day, or neglect his child for days at a time and then make up for it with a Saturday morning frolic at the park, is deceiving himself.

Your children need your love and attention constantly. Quality time is important, yes, but so is the amount of time you give your children. Taking the time to be with them—whether it's just sitting and talking, playing a board game, or going out to a ball game together—tells them that you really do value them. And your children need to know that they are important to you.

Before anyone jumps down my throat and tells me I'm placing impossible demands on parents, let me explain that I do understand how difficult it can be to find time to spend with your children. Yes, I understand that many mothers have to work to help make ends meet. And I understand that many fathers have to work overtime, or have to go out of town on business trips. All I'm saying is that spending time with your children ought to be very high on your list of priorities.

Believe me, I understand how things can be. I am frequently called upon to lead seminars, to lecture, to appear on various television shows, and sometimes I am gone from home for a week

72

at a time. When I'm on the road, I certainly can't be spending time with my children. There's nothing I can do about it, with the exception of frequent phone calls home and, of course, keeping them in my prayers.

But when I'm home I do everything I can to catch up on what's been going on in their lives while I've been gone, and I demonstrate my love for them by spending as much time as possible with them.

(A word of caution, though: Your children should never be higher on your list of priorities than your relationship with your spouse. Don't spend time with your children at the expense of time with your mate. A marriage must be built around the love and respect between a man and a woman, and not around their relationship with their children.)

I think it's important not to limit time spent with your children to doing things as a group. Each child needs your individual one-on-one attention.

I can hear someone ask: "Well, Dr. Leman—I have five children. How in the world am I going to be able to spend one-on-one time with each of them?"

You'll make time, and when you do, it really pays off. Our five children, from age thirty-four down to fourteen, still want to hang out with us. We have a summer home in New York State, and everybody—including our married daughter Krissy, husband Dennis, and their two children—all make the effort to come back to New York State. Our son Kevin, a comedy writer and producer on the *Ellen* TV show, and daughters Holly and Hannah make an equal effort to "hang out" with their parents.

If your schedule is such that you think you can't spend that much time with your children, the best thing for you to do is rearrange your schedule.

One acquaintance of mine had an extremely tight schedule. He spent as much time with his three children as he possibly could, but he knew it wasn't enough.

So he got out his calendar and looked at his schedule for the next three months. By shifting a few things around here and there, he was able to completely clear the decks for one Saturday each month.

He then told each of his three children to decide what they would really like to do on their particular Saturday.

The older son wanted to go fishing from a boat.

Now the father didn't know anything at all about fishing. And, in fact, he told me that he doesn't even like to eat fish. The final complication was that he didn't have a boat or know anyone else who did, even though the family lived within five miles of the ocean.

He could have said, "Look, son, that's not really such a great idea. Why don't you find something a little more realistic."' But instead of doing that, he viewed the fishing expedition as an adventure—as a chance to try his hand at something new.

Checking around, he found a local company that sent fishing boats out every Saturday morning at seven. The cost was only ten dollars apiece, and for two dollars more, they would supply you with rods and reels. Father and son ended up having a great time. Dad's only regret, in fact, was that his boy brought home more fish than he did. Neither one of them was crazy about scaling and cleaning the fish, but they did it, and even that was a new, shared experience which helped to bring them closer together.

The next month, the eleven-year-old daughter had decided that her big day would be . . . can you guess? That's right, a fun day shopping at the mall to be followed by dinner in a fancy restaurant.

Dad quickly began counting his money, figuring that a day at the mall could easily set him back a week's pay—not to mention that fancy restaurant afterward. (And then, there aren't too many men who look forward to spending several hours in a shopping mall.)

But his daughter told him that she didn't really care about buying lots of things. She just liked to look—at clothes, books, music, and sometimes she liked to sit on a bench in the middle of the mall and watch the boys go by. As far as a "fancy" restaurant was concerned, all she really meant was somewhere where you actually sat down and looked at a menu, and where the food was brought to your table.

Dad was surprised when his day in the mall turned out to be a delight. He laughed more than he had in years. He and his daughter had fun looking in the stores, they acted silly, they shared ice-cream sundaes in the food area, and especially enjoyed picking out small, inexpensive presents to take home to the other members of the family. Then they capped off their big day with an exclusive dinner of fried chicken and French fries. (They were looking out for their emotional health a bit more than they were their physical health, what with sundaes and fried foods!)

When the youngest child's time came, all he wanted to do was to go see the latest movie featuring his favorite animated hero. After that, he favored a trip to the neighborhood pizza parlor.

Once again, Dad would have opted for something a bit more exciting—but this was his son's day, and if that's what the boy really wanted to do, that was fine with him. After all, he wouldn't have picked a fishing trip nor a day at the mall.

This day, too, turned out to be a good one. Dad found himself chuckling at the cartoon, and he and his son shared sodas and popcorn. Afterward, at the pizza parlor, they talked about the movie and went back over their favorite parts.

Now, the truth is that nothing earthshaking happened on any of those three days. And from a purely practical standpoint, it wasn't easy for Dad to crowd the work he normally did on Saturdays into the other days of the week.

But you can be sure that he'll always remember those special times spent with the children, and so will they. What's more he's vowed to continue the practice of giving each of his children "special days." The outcome of these days will not only be happy memories, but children who have a sense of their own importance in the eyes of their father. With this sort of parental love, they will not grow up to be defeated perfectionists.

I cannot overstress the importance of this. Find time to be with your children. Talk to them. Find out what's on their minds. Learn to enjoy them.

There are several things you can do to open and develop good lines of communication between parents and children. These are important, because without communication, time spent together doesn't really accomplish anything. Too many parents don't know how to communicate with their children, and the situation seems to be getting worse.

In her book *The Plug-In Drug*, author Marie Winn tells about the effect television in particular has had upon communication within families. She paints a picture, supported by various surveys, of families sitting around a television set for hours at a time, but without engaging in any form of communication. She quotes a nurse from the pediatrics ward of a hospital who would see parents sitting in embarrassed silence at the bedsides of their children, obviously looking for something to say, but not knowing where or how to begin.[4]

Spending quality time with your children includes talking and listening to them.

You can bring about better communication if you will follow the suggestions listed below.[5]

1. Think before you speak. Nothing gets in the way of communication like coming on too strong, responding to a child's request in a threatening way, or jumping down his throat. If your son comes to you and asks you if he can have a motorcycle, don't respond by yelling, "What? Are you crazy! Of course you can't have a motorcycle! Don't you know how dangerous those things are!" You may be dead set against your son getting a motorcycle, but take a few moments to reflect and think before you answer him. And he will be more apt to listen to you if you start off the conversation by saying something like, "I can see that motorcycles are exciting, but what worries me about them is that they're so dangerous." Your son may not like your final answer any more than he would if you jumped all over him about wanting a motorcycle, but he'll be more apt to at least listen to you, and to know that you and he can have a relational discussion about such matters.

2. Stress the positive. Say you've been to a Powder Puff softball game and your daughter got two hits, but she also struck out with the bases loaded and dropped a fly ball. You stress the positive by saying something like, "You seemed to be having a good time out there today. You played well and you really socked that ball a couple of times." There's no need at all for you to bring up the "less successful aspects" of the game.

3. Deal with the negative in a positive, matter-of-fact way. If, for instance, your daughter responds to comments about her game by saying, "Yeah, but I struck out with the bases loaded," you can say something like, "Well, nobody gets a base hit every time up. But if you keep practicing, I'll bet that pitcher won't strike you out again!"

4. Remember to communicate your love and care. Even if your child is angry and sarcastic, do your best not to respond in kind. "Listen, I know you're upset, but I love you and it makes me unhappy when you talk to me that way. Let's not talk this way to each other, even if we are angry, okay?" Or suppose you have just yelled at your three-year-old because she was about to stick a screwdriver into an electrical outlet. "Mommy yelled at you because what you were doing could have caused you to be hurt, and I would be very sad if that happened." Be sure that you're doing your best to explain that your actions are prompted by your love for the child.

5. Don't be afraid to admit your mistakes. Asking for forgiveness is never easy, especially when you have to humble yourself in front of your children. But when you do make a mistake—jump to the wrong conclusion or refuse to listen to a child's point of view—you must be able to own up to it and say that you are sorry. When you apologize to your children it helps to establish better lines of communication, but it also teaches them how to face up to their own mistakes and seek forgiveness from those they have wronged. The defeated perfectionist comes to believe that his life is one gigantic mistake after another, and that there is no way to overcome his error-prone ways. He grows up wondering why he always had so much trouble doing the right thing. He most likely didn't have a parent who was capable of apologizing, of showing him that, hey, even mothers and fathers can make mistakes and it's not the end of the world. A statement such as "I really owe you an apology" or "I want to tell you I really used poor judgment in this matter" won't diminish you in the eyes of your child. Instead, it will add to the respect he feels for you.

6. Realize that some things don't change overnight. Anything worthwhile takes time and effort, and that's true when it comes to establishing communication with your kids. If communication hasn't been good, chances are that they will not decide, all of a sudden, to start opening up with you and carrying on a deep dialogue. You must continuously work at keeping the lines of communication open and demonstrate that your willingness to listen and discuss things calmly and rationally is not a passing fad.

7. Ask for God's guidance. Anyone who thinks he can be an effective parent without a large daily dose of prayer is mistaken. My own personal prayer is that my life would be such that my children would see the reality of my personal relationship with God. This is extremely important for a variety of reasons, not the least of which is that the defeated perfectionist often has a difficult time establishing his own relationship with God. He finds it hard to believe that God really loves him and cares about him. Or, because he has such a hard time forgiving himself for his own sins—real and imagined—it's hard for him to accept the fact that God could forgive him. A healthy prayer life and demonstration of a proper relationship with the Almighty will go a long way toward building healthy self-esteem in your children.

If your own relationship with God isn't in order, I suggest that you take time to ponder just what that relationship ought to be. Remember that parents who see themselves as unworthy and undeserving tend to make the cycle go around. They will produce children who see themselves as unworthy and undeserving, who will also produce children who see themselves as unworthy and undeserving—and the perpetual cycle of defeated perfectionists goes round and round forever!

So now we've seen three rungs on the ladder that leads to confident, productive adulthood—patience, encouragement, and giving of parental time and energy. It's easy to see, too, that there are certain areas where these characteristics overlap. For instance, if you have patience, you will take the time and energy necessary to encourage your children. The fourth rung on the ladder to respectable, responsible adulthood is called "reality discipline," and it, too, involves the other three rungs.

Reality discipline, to put it in the simplest possible terms, means allowing your child to be responsible for his own actions, in a way that makes the reality of the situation at hand become the teacher to the child.

Responsibility is something that defeated perfectionists seldom learn. The person who lives in a world of defeat and rejection is responsible for everything and nothing at the same time. What do I mean by that? Well, the defeated perfectionist is quick to accept the blame—"Oh, it's my fault," or, "I blew it again," are two of his favorite expressions. He'll tell you he's sorry for anything and everything that happens, whether or not it was really his fault.

But he's never really learned to face up to his true responsibilities and, once he's failed, to be able to do something about it.

Reality discipline says that if I am always bailing my children out, they will never learn to be able to stand on their own two feet. They will always be looking for someone to pull them out of the jam. That may work all right when you're seven years old and Mom is close at hand. But it's not going to solve anything if you're thirty-five and working for an accounting firm!

The Ladder to Responsible Adulthood

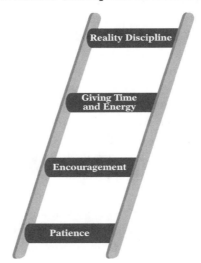

Love Is Not Enough

I've been asked my opinion regarding the biggest mistake parents can make. And even though there are literally thousands of mistakes we can make—and *do* make—in the rearing of our children, the biggest one is simply this: thinking that if I love my children enough, they're going to grow up right; that they'll just naturally turn out to be solid, productive citizens.

Believe me, I've counseled many disillusioned parents who tell me, "I don't understand it! Nobody could have loved little Johnny (or Joanie) as much as I did, and I can't understand how he could do this to me!" Johnny may be a teenager who's decided to dye his spiked hair blue and put a safety pin through his cheek, or he may be a thirty-year-old corporate executive who doesn't want anything to do with his parents because he's too involved with his own selfish life.

There's nothing in the world like love. But love must be much more than feelings of tenderness and joy. Love must include reality discipline.

I know it's not easy to practice reality discipline. No parent wants to see his child in a difficult situation, especially when you know you have the power to pull him out of it. Very often reality discipline brings out the truth in that old cliché which has been used by fathers and mothers for centuries: "This is going to hurt me worse than it hurts you."

For instance, suppose eleven-year-old Judy has been saving for several weeks to buy herself a special jacket—the sort the most popular girls in school are wearing. She's so proud of the jacket and can't wait to show it off at school.

For the first few days she wears it everywhere, even when the weather is better suited to short sleeves. Then one afternoon she comes in without it.

"Where's your jacket?"

"Oh, I left it over at Cindy's."

"Hadn't you better go get it?"

She thinks for a moment and then says, "Oh, it'll be okay. I'll get it tomorrow."

You figure the jacket is safe at Cindy's so you let it go. But the next day, Judy comes home from school with a panicked look on her face, flops down on the couch, and begins sobbing.

It takes her several minutes to get the story out through her tears, but she finally manages to tell you this story: She stopped by Cindy's on her way to school, but the jacket wasn't there.

Cindy's mom says she wasn't wearing a jacket when she came by yesterday, and that maybe she left it at school. Only it wasn't at school, and she looked everywhere. She remembered that she stopped by the park yesterday after school, and maybe she left it there. But now it isn't there. If it's not at school, not at the park, and not at Cindy's, it must be gone! That loss, of course, is almost more than she can bear, because that jacket meant the world to her.

Naturally, you're going to be angry that Judy was so irresponsible as to leave her jacket lying around where anyone could have taken it. But then you realize that she saved up to buy it, and you see how sad and unhappy she is, and your heart really goes out to her.

Well, actually, the jacket wasn't all that expensive. You could get her another one without thinking twice about it. Is that what you should do?

Reality discipline says that it isn't. If Judy saved up to buy the jacket before, she can save up enough to buy a replacement. It won't be easy on her, but it will teach her that she must be responsible and take care of her possessions. You can bet that she will be much more careful with her next jacket.

I talked earlier about children who have to be told over and over to do anything. This is another situation where reality discipline comes into play.

Bobby, who is ten, is one of those boys who never comes the first time he is called.

"Bobby, dinner's ready!"

Nothing.

Five minutes later you try again. "Bobby, I said dinner is ready. Please come to the table!"

Still nothing.

Another five minutes pass, the food is getting cold, and there is still no sign of Bobby—only the blips and bleeps from a computer game emitting from his room.

"BOBBY," you finally yell, in a voice so loud it rattles windows on the other side of town, "GET YOURSELF IN HERE RIGHT NOW!"

At this, Bobby finally knows that you mean business, and he turns off his game and comes to the table. Only by this time, you're "ticked," and dinnertime is going to be anything but pleasant.

Once again, reality discipline must come into play in this situation. Bobby should be called to dinner once. If he doesn't show up, Mom and Dad should go ahead and eat.

When Bobby finally wanders into the kitchen, he is surprised to discover that Mom and Dad are already clearing the dishes from the table.

"I'm sorry, Bobby," you tell him, "but I called you to dinner and you didn't come. We've finished eating, so if you're hungry you'll have to help yourself."

Or, if he shows up ten minutes into the meal, you say, "I'm sorry, Bobby, but you're just going to have to wait until the rest of us are through eating. If you want something, you'll have to fix it for yourself later."

If Bobby's stubborn and doesn't want to fix anything for himself, then he just goes hungry. It won't hurt him. And it will teach him that you mean business when you call him to the table.

One woman found it nearly impossible to drag her twelve-year-old son out of bed in the morning. She'd wake him up, and he'd sit up and tell her he was going to get dressed. But then, after another ten minutes or so had passed, she'd find him back in bed sound asleep. This went on day after day, with the result that the boy would have to run out the door every morning in a frantic footrace to catch his school bus.

He missed it about one day a week, which meant that Mom or Dad had to drive him to school. And, since both parents worked, they didn't have much time to spend serving as their son's personal driver.

When Mom came into contact with reality discipline, she realized that she had been handling this problem the wrong way. It was her son's responsibility to get up and get ready for school.

She sat down with him and explained that she was through dragging him out of bed. She was supplying him with an alarm clock, and she expected him to use it. From then on, he would be responsible for getting up when he was supposed to, and if he missed the bus, he would have to walk to school.

Well, sure enough, the very first day of the new game plan, the boy turned the alarm off and went back to sleep. Mom stood firm, though, and when her son was finally ready, she handed him his lunch money and told him to have a good day.

"But aren't you going to take me?" he whined.

"No, I'm not. You know we talked about this."

"But I'll be late to first bell."

"I'm sorry but you and I have an agreement. You are either going to have to learn how to get out of bed in the morning, or you're going to face the consequences."

"But it's cold."

Well, it wasn't that cold, and Mom—good for her—wasn't going to let herself be talked out of her new strategy. There was no, "Oh, well, I guess I can take you just one more time. But you'd better get yourself ready on time tomorrow." Her son may have thought at the time that she was being arbitrary and cruel, but she knew that she was doing what was best for him.

There were several mornings after this when the boy ran out the door just in time to catch the bus, and there were a few more times when he had to walk to school. But slowly and surely things improved. It wasn't long before he was doing a masterful job of getting up when the alarm went off. He was even having time to sit down and enjoy a good breakfast before heading out to catch the bus. As for Mom, one of the things she had hated most in her routine was dragging that boy out of bed every morning. Now that she doesn't have to do that anymore, her day gets off to a better start, and that gives her a better attitude, which makes for a better relationship with her husband and son.

Does reality discipline sound harsh? Does it sound narrow and confining? It isn't.

Actually, it frees up the children and the parents. They all understand what is expected of them, and they also understand the consequences of not fulfilling their obligations.

Dr. James Dobson tells about a school where it was decided that fences around the playground would be torn down because they were too confining. School officials wanted the children to have a sense of freedom.

But then, after the fences were gone, they noticed something. At recess, all of the children stayed close together in the center of the playground. As long as the fences had been up, they had felt secure enough to scatter all over the playground, even to the point of climbing upon the fences. But without the fences there to define their limits, they were timid and afraid.[6]

My point is that children do need to know where they stand. They need to know what their responsibilities are, and exactly what Mom and Dad expect of them—even if they act as if they don't appreciate it. They may climb on the fences from time to time, but they don't really want those fences to be removed.

There are three other things I've learned about reality discipline over the years.

1. *Never use reality discipline as an excuse to force your child to do more than he or she can do.* As your child grows, his capabilities increase. You couldn't expect a five-year-old to get himself out of bed and get ready for school in the morning without a little help from mom or dad. But it's certainly not too much to expect a twelve-year-old to get himself ready. Reality discipline must be combined with an understanding of the child's abilities and inabilities.

2. *Hold your child accountable, but don't apply unnecessary pressure.* How do you know if you're applying too much pressure? The only way is to be sensitive, to listen to your child, and to keep the lines of communication open.

3. *Using reality discipline can cut both ways.* This means that it takes into account the reality of your child's weaknesses and fears. Reality discipline must always be administered with a heaping helping of love.[7]

Another hallmark of reality discipline is that it keeps short accounts.[8] This means that it is a "case by case" form of discipline, and it is also an "on the spot" type of discipline.

It is "case by case" in that there is no room in reality discipline for allowing anger and resentment to fester. There is no room for statements such as, "You always do this," or "Just wait until your father gets home." Your child needs to know that whenever he breaks a rule or engages in any type of misbehavior, he is putting reality discipline into action.

He needs to know, too, as closely as he can, what reality discipline is going to involve. He shouldn't be forced to guess what his punishment will be, hoping that Dad is in a good mood today so it will be light, nor should he be forced to wait around for hours while his fate is debated.

What you are striving for with reality discipline is getting your child to see and understand what he has done wrong, offering him an opportunity to repent of his actions, and seeing to it that he knows he has been dealt with fairly.

You must remember that you are not punishing your child, nor are you simply trying to make him toe the mark. Instead, what you are out to do is to help your child become a responsible adult who will exercise realistic self-control and self-discipline.

In my book *Making Children Mind Without Losing Yours*, I list five distinctives of reality discipline, and I believe they are worth repeating here.

1. Parents never seek to punish; they always seek to discipline, train, and teach.
2. If "punishment," pain, or some kind of consequence is involved, the parent is not doing it or causing it—reality is. . . .

3. Reality Discipline is the best system I know to avoid inconsistent meandering between authoritarianism and permissiveness.
4. Reality Discipline is the best system for teaching accountability and responsibility in a way that will stick. . . .
5. Above all, Reality Discipline is your best bet for avoiding what I call the Super Parent Syndrome.[9]

What exactly is the Super Parent Syndrome? To put it as succinctly as possible, it's the attitude of parents that:

1. I own my children.
2. I am judge and jury.
3. My children can't fail.
4. I am boss—what I say goes.[10]

This kind of authoritarian parenting seldom works. It's not fair for the children involved, and it's not fair for the parents, who feel personally responsible for making sure that their children toe the line in everything they do.

A child who is reared in this sort of environment may seem to walk the straight and narrow, but he's doing it out of fear, not because he's learned responsibility and knows what's best for him. A child who is produced by authoritarian parenting will normally head in one of two ways when he reaches adulthood.

Most likely, he'll become the defeated perfectionist, someone who can never find fulfillment and who always feels as if someone is looking over his shoulder, judging him. Or, he'll go the other way, and as soon as he is out on his own he'll get involved in all sorts of wild living, simply because he wants to show the world that "Hey, I'm free of parental control at last!"

If you want to see kids go totally wild, spend a few days on a college campus. More specifically, spend a few days on a college campus watching the young men and women who have been raised in severely authoritarian homes. Because they have never had to discipline themselves, they're not about to start now, and the result is often utter chaos and eventual heartbreak for the students and their parents.

Get Started . . . Now

Now suppose you haven't been doing right by your children. You haven't been patient and encouraging, you haven't given of your time and energy, and you haven't been using reality discipline. You say, "Dr. Leman, you said that the first few years of a child's life are absolutely crucial. My children are already in their teens. Does that mean it's too late for me to start doing things right?"

My answer is that it's never too late to get on the right path. Naturally, it would have been better if you had been doing all the right things from the start, but no parent is perfect and we all make plenty of mistakes.

No matter how old your children are, you can start doing things right. And you should start off by sitting down with them and apologizing. Tell them that you've been doing things wrong, but you're going to change your ways.

For example, in the case of the woman who decided to stop dragging her son out of bed, she had to say something like this:

"I'm sorry that I've been dragging you out of bed every morning and practically forcing you out the door. I'm sorry because that hasn't been fair to you. It hasn't let you show me that you're capable of being responsible for yourself, and it hasn't helped to teach you self-discipline. So from now on, things are going to change."

If you haven't been spending enough time with your child, you might say something like, "You know, I've decided that I've been spending too much time at the office, and I'm sorry. From now on, I'm going to get home a little earlier so we'll have time for a game of catch before dinner. And I'm going to keep Sunday afternoons open so we can spend some time together."

One other extremely important thing. Once you've said something such as that, stick to it. If you've decided to exercise reality discipline, don't let yourself be talked out of it. If you promise to spend more time with your son or daughter, don't go back on it. It may be a cliché, but it's true that actions speak louder than words—especially when it comes to children.

We've spent a long time now talking about steps you can take to insure that your children don't grow up to be defeated perfectionists, drowning in a sea of self-rejection.

But what about you? What if you grew up in a home where your parents didn't exercise patience and encouragement, where they had little or no time for you and didn't know the first thing about reality discipline?

Perhaps you feel scarred and bent. Is it too late for you to change things and begin to feel more at ease with yourself and your role in this world? Can anything be done?

The answer is yes, something can be done. You can overcome the doubts and fears brought on by an unhappy childhood—and we'll talk about that next.

Part 2

Discovering Who You Really Are

4

The Critical Parent and You

Margaret is forty years old. She's a refined woman who enjoys the better things in life. She's tall, statuesque, with silky black hair and luminous green eyes—a very pretty woman. She loves to entertain and prides herself on being a gourmet cook. She and her husband live in a tastefully furnished four-bedroom house in an upper-middle-class area of the city.

When you first meet her, she makes you wish you could have things together as well as she does. Yes, indeed, Margaret is a study in calm, cool, and collected.

Until, that is, her mother comes to town for a visit.

"I don't understand it," she says. "I'm panicked for days before she gets here. I dust and polish, and polish some more. No matter how hard I try, I can't get the house looking the way I want it.

"And it's true, too. As soon as she walks through the door, she finds something wrong. It's either 'Oh, my dear, you really need to paint these walls,' or, 'I'm sure you're so busy you don't have a lot of time for housework.'"

Margaret even recalls one occasion when her mother hadn't been in the house for more than half an hour when she got the vacuum cleaner out of the closet and went to work on the downstairs carpet, "and it was already spotless."

Deep down inside Margaret knows that her mother is being arbitrary and overly critical. She knows the house is clean. She knows the carpet doesn't really need to be vacuumed, and yet, there is a part of her that believes everything her mother says about her.

"She hasn't been with me for more than a couple of hours before I start thinking that I'm nothing but a failure—like I can't keep house or cook, and that my husband and children really must suffer putting up with the likes of me."

It doesn't take too long for her mother's nitpicking to become a self-fulfilling prophecy either. Margaret tries to give a dinner party in honor of her mother's stay, but nothing turns out right. Of course, that's partly because Mother insists on following her around in the kitchen making "suggestions" about the way her daughter is doing things. As a result, the meat is burned, the fancy dessert looks and tastes like glue, and nobody—but nobody—seems to have a good time.

Says Margaret: "It's always been this way, ever since I was a tiny little girl. I could never do anything right as far as she was concerned. I remember her laughing at me and saying, 'Margaret, you're just hopeless . . . hopeless!' And that's how she makes me feel now. Like a hopeless, helpless little girl."

Margaret says she loves her mother—at least she's trying awfully hard. Because she lives nearly a thousand miles from her mother, they see each other only once each year, when Mom comes for her annual two-week visit. Those two weeks are sheer agony for Margaret, who seems to dread it more each year.

"I'm just grateful that we don't live closer to each other," she sighs.

Then there's David, who is thirty-five and the father of three children. The complaint isn't his, but his wife's. Bobbi says that

David simply refuses to help her discipline their children. In fact, more often than not, he'll take their side against her, accusing her of being too harsh, or reminding her that "boys will be boys."

"He never takes my side," she says, "and whenever I really need to confront one of the kids about something, he'll walk out of the room and leave everything up to me.

"All I get from the kids is, 'Dad doesn't care, so why should you?'"

The kids are wrong, of course. David does care, but he doesn't know what to do about it. Like Margaret, David grew up in a house where his parents were biting and critical of everything he did.

Whereas Margaret was being called "hopeless," David's mother and father were more into words like *stupid* and *idiot*. In fact, he remembers that his father's long suit was superlatives. Whenever David fouled up, it was always the "worst" thing he could have done, or he was the "stupidest" boy in the world. He remembers that his mother worked six days a week to help make ends meet, and he realizes looking back on it that being overworked probably was largely responsible for her bitter mood.

"But I used to dread her coming home in the evening. It seemed like she'd start yelling as soon as she walked in the house. I'd try my best to get the house cleaned up for her, and to keep my little sister out of mischief—but there was always something."

He shakes his head slowly and flashes a quick smile as if the situation has suddenly become quite funny. "I'd be willing to wager," he says, "that if the *Guinness Book of World Records* had a category for 'Most Days in a Row Yelled At,' my name would be at the top of the list."

What does David's childhood have to do with his inability to discipline his children? Everything.

"I can't stand it when Bobbi yells at the kids," he says.

"I don't yell at them," she counters.

"I know you don't. But to me it seems like you do. I don't really know how to explain it, but whenever you have to speak to one of them about something, I always hear my mother yelling at me.

"You say something like, 'I've told you before not to leave your bike in the middle of the driveway,' and I hear it as, 'You're the stupidest boy in the world.' I know you don't *say* it, but I *think* you're going to say it and it really hurts me. I remember how hurt I always was when my parents talked to me like that, and I just don't want our kids to hurt that way."

David understands that children must be disciplined. He wants to take a more active role, but in order to do that, he has to throw off the chains that were wrapped around him during his childhood by a sharp-tongued father and a nagging mother.

And what about Margaret? Will she ever be able to rid herself of her own insecurities, and let her mother's critical remarks bounce off her? David can overcome and so can Margaret, but it will not be done easily, with a snap of the fingers.

Parents who are always critical of their children are inflicting damage in several ways. It is very rare for those who grew up in this sort of atmosphere to be perfectly adjusted, well-rounded adults—even if they give that appearance. Such children invariably grow up to be defeated perfectionists, always seeking perfection but knowing they'll never get there because they're stupid, lazy, crazy, bad, and all of those other things their parents told them they were.

Most often, a person who grows up in an unpleasant, perpetually critical atmosphere will become an unpleasant, perpetually critical adult. His problem, primarily, is that he feels insecure and full of self-hatred so he hides it by lashing out at those around him—or perhaps by tearing them apart he hopes to bring them down to his level.

Others, like David, will go so far in the opposite direction that they will go to any lengths to avoid confrontation. They become what I call "pleasers" and often wind up married to domineering spouses who control every aspect of their lives.[1]

I don't care who you are, it's bound to be hard on you when someone criticizes you. You may laugh and attempt to shrug it off, but deep down inside, it hurts.

I remember, for instance, getting a negative letter from a woman who had read one of my books on rearing children. Now, I've received negative mail before, but this one was the hate letter to end all hate letters. The writer didn't like the concept of reality discipline and thought I was being much too harsh when I suggested that children should face up to the consequences of their own actions.

My daughter Holly was ten years old at the time, and the first line of the letter was, "I wish your ten-year-old would kick your teeth out." Well, that certainly wasn't the nicest greeting I had ever received, and it made me angry. I felt that my integrity had been challenged, my intelligence questioned, and I didn't like it one bit.

It was my wife, Sande, who finally gave me a bit of very good advice. "You know," she said, "It's easy to love people who think you're wonderful, but it's hard to love those who think you're a jerk."

She was right, of course. It is hard to love people who don't think highly of you. Now, I had known, ever since I was a small child, that Jesus Christ commanded us to love our enemies (Luke 6:27), and I had always given a vague assent to that, agreeing that yes, of course, this was the way it ought to be—but this letter writer was really putting me to the test. Sande's pointed comment made me understand that this was exactly what I had to do—love the person who had written this letter and consider whether there was any validity to her criticism. If there wasn't, I could disregard it and realize that the problem lay with the letter writer, and not with me.

My point, though, is this: If unkind words from a total stranger can cut us to the core, imagine what unkind words from a mother or father can do.

Here are several things you must remember if you seek to overcome the damage inflicted by critical parents:

1. Some people are born critics and complainers.
2. You don't have to believe everything your parents told (or tell) you.
3. You can't please some people no matter what you do. (So don't spend too much time worrying about vindicating yourself.)
4. You must understand why you feel the way you do.
5. You must exercise what I call "cognitive self-discipline."

Let's take a closer look at these five items.

The Natural-Born Complainer

The plain truth is, some people are going to criticize you no matter what you do.

I can't think of a better example of this than the way people treated Jesus Christ during His years of ministry. No one ever lived a better, more loving, more beneficial life than He did. And yet He was the subject of criticism, ridicule, and scorn to the point where jeering crowds demanded His crucifixion. If He couldn't escape rejection and criticism, then you and I certainly aren't going to escape it either.

When we talk about dealing with criticism, two stories come to mind.

The first is an ancient parable about a man and his son who were traveling along a dusty road with their donkey, taking bags full of produce from their farm into the city.

First of all, the father led the donkey along while the boy rode on the animal's back. But as they traveled along that way, they overheard the sarcastic remarks of strangers who said, "Look at that! The lazy boy rides while his poor father walks."

This bothered them, so they decided to switch positions. The boy got down and the father got up on the donkey's back. But this didn't please anyone either. Now they said, "What a cruel man—making his son walk while he takes it easy."

Well, what could they do? Perhaps they should both ride on the donkey's back. And of course when they tried that, people said, "Look at that poor donkey! How could they expect that poor animal to carry both of them and the rest of the load he's carrying, too."

In a last attempt to please people, the man and his son dismounted and both walked along in front of the beast. Did that help? Of course not.

Now they heard people laughing and saying, "Look at those stupid people. Here they have a perfectly healthy donkey! At least one of them should be riding, but instead they both walk."

Well, this old, apocryphal tale has a very good moral to it. You can't please everybody no matter what you do, and if you try you're only going to end up confused and tired!

The other story, a bit more modern, concerns a couple of friends who were out at the lake, duck hunting. One of the men, Ralph, was always bragging about his wonderful bird dogs—they were absolutely the best in the world.

But the other hunter, Harold, had a special surprise in store for his friend today. He had a new dog, a very special dog, which could do something no other dog could do.

It wasn't long before the first ducks of the day flew over and—blam! blam!—Harold got two of them, which fell into the center of the lake.

"Go get them, boy!" he said to his dog.

At that, the dog took off into the lake. But instead of swimming, he ran along right on top of the water, just as if he were running on dry ground.

He picked up the ducks in his mouth, and then ran back to his master, without getting anything but his paws wet. Harold was sure that this time he had beaten Ralph at his own game. But instead, all Ralph did was shake his head sadly.

"Some dog," he sneered. "Can't even swim."

Well, the story would be funnier if it weren't so painfully true to life. Some people simply cannot find anything nice to say about anyone or anything. What's more, they can't seem to keep their mouths shut about it. It wouldn't be so bad if they'd just keep their opinions to themselves, but they insist on sharing them with others.

And some people take a special delight in telling us what's wrong with ourselves. These are the pests who insist on telling you if they think your blouse doesn't quite match with your skirt, or if you're suffering from "ring around the collar." Of course, it's always for your own good. They're just trying to be helpful. But they aren't, really. Real friends do, however, tell you when you have something hanging out of your nose—or your fly is wide open!

It's all a matter of motive, of course. A really close friend might be seeking to do you a favor by telling you that your tie didn't go with your pants or that you had a spot on the back of your blouse. But there are those who either delight in criticizing for criticizing's sake, or else who are always seeking to bring others down to their level.

Things they say might not come across as harsh and judgmental upon first glance. They are minor, "constructive" criticisms—a long, long line of "constructive" criticisms. Sometimes this "I just want to help" form of criticism is worse than having someone tell you to your face that he thinks you're a dummy.

Why? Because, with that second type of person, at least you know where you stand, and you can tell that he is hostile toward you. The person who pretends to want to help you, but who can't stop picking at you, trying to change you, and rolling his eyes heavenward when you foul up again—that person can have a profound effect on your self-esteem.

The sooner you realize that some people are just naturally picky and critical, and that not everyone has your best interest at heart, the better off you will be.

Even My Parents?

Yes, even your parents may be this way. And that brings us to the second point: You don't have to believe everything your parents tell you.

Does this sound like blasphemy? Well, believe me, I might hesitate to say it if I hadn't seen so many cases of people, like Margaret and David, who were deeply hurt through lies their parents told them.

Lies may take the form of prophetic utterances, such as "You'll never amount to anything," or, "I can't wait until you leave home so your father and I can travel." (This last lie, by the way, is a great favorite of mothers and fathers, and varieties of it have been used for at least a hundred years. You can use it as a "fill-in-the-blanks" line: Such as, "I can't wait until you leave home so: a. We can travel; b. We can have decent furniture; c. We can have a neat house; d. We can have some peace and quiet around here" . . . and so on. If you grew up in a home with a parent who liked to use this line, you can probably think of ten or fifteen more examples.)

Or the lies may take the more subtle form of constant nitpicking and "correcting." "It's for your own good!"

This may involve a barrage of comments such as, "Sit up straight, dear, men don't like girls with poor posture," and, "You'd better eat those turnips, because you'll never find a wife if you don't."

A friend of mine shared with me that he was actually afraid he would never get married but would wind up a sad and lonely old man, simply because he wouldn't eat turnips and black-eyed peas. The assumption, apparently, was that all women love cooking turnips and black-eyed peas, and you'll never find a woman who could agree to give up fixing them. Yes, I agree, that's about the dumbest thing I've ever heard. But the point is that as a young boy, he believed it—and when you get right down to it, it's no "dumber" than a lot of other lies about ourselves that some of us have believed, whether they came from our parents or anyone else.

It could have been that your parents were (or are) among the ranks of the chronic complainers and fault finders. But, because our parents are so important to us—because we depend upon them to protect us, teach us, and provide for us—it is harder to see that their motives may not always be the best. Or, because parents are older and wiser than we are, it may be hard to see that the things they say and do are not always proper and beneficial. That's why criticism and condemnation from parents has such a profound effect on us. It's much harder to deal with than criticism from siblings or friends.

Take a few moments to reflect back on your relationship with your parents. Were they forever criticizing and correcting you? If so, how did it make you feel?

After you've thought about that for a while, ask yourself how you relate to your own children. Are you passing along the cycle of rejection and discouragement to them? If you are, resolve to stop it. Then, as we discussed in the last chapter, sit down with your children and apologize to them. Tell them you've been wrong in your attitude and your actions, and it's not going to continue. Tell them you realize that you might slip up once in a while, but you're going to do your best to change your ways. As I mentioned earlier, admitting your own shortcomings to your children is usually a good idea. For one thing, it encourages them to know that you love them enough to let your guard down and really be yourself in front of them. For another, the fact that even Mom or Dad can make mistakes, and then admit to them, will make them feel better about their own failures and shortcomings. Of course, some things are personal and should remain so.

If you see that you have been caught up in a whirlpool of rejection and discouragement, beginning with your relationship with your parents, then take action now to stop it before your children—and then your grandchildren, and your great-grandchildren after them—are sucked into the whirling mess.

Now, as a Christian, I do believe in the Ten Commandments, including the one that says to honor your father and mother (Exod. 20:12). And I am not advocating here that you don't have to honor your father and mother, or that your children don't have to honor you. But honoring your parents does not include believing lies they tell you, no matter what those lies may be.

You may remember in George Orwell's *1984* how the state sought to drive its authority home by insisting that the correct answer to the equation two-plus-two was five. When the hero, Winston, insisted that the correct answer to two-plus-two was four, he was told that if the state said the correct answer was five, the correct answer *was* five, end of discussion.[2]

Well, I don't care how many times the state, or your parents, or anybody else tells you that two-plus-two is five, that still isn't the truth, and you don't have to believe it.

If your parents told you that grass was red and the sky was green, you wouldn't be expected to believe them. Neither should you believe the lies they tell you about yourself—even if those lies are unintentional or well-meaning.

I have known of cases where parents continually pointed at the Ten Commandments in an effort to keep their children in line.

"Do you know what the Bible says? It says to honor your father and mother. That means you'd better listen to me when I'm talking to you!"

But I've never believed the Bible should or could be used as a club, whether by a parent, a preacher, or anyone else. And I would remind anyone who is offended by what I've said about not having to believe everything your parents tell you that the Bible also warns fathers against provoking their children by constantly picking at them (Eph. 6:4).

God's plan is for mutual respect and consideration: children honoring their parents, and parents, in turn, loving their children and treating them with the respect they deserve as creatures made in the image of God.

I don't care if you're sixteen or fifty-six, it is still possible that you are bound up with feelings of inadequacy and worthlessness because of lies your parents have told you. Don't misunderstand and think that I'm telling you that you should openly challenge your parents and say something like, "That's not true, and I don't believe it." You don't have to provoke open warfare. But you can resolve to disregard these lies and half-truths and remember that they have nothing to do with you, nor with your worth as a human being.

Whenever you are evaluating a criticism about yourself always consider three things:

1. The words used.
2. The source.
3. The moment.

If you'll listen to the words, and the way they are used, you'll begin to hear the lies about you. Words such as *you always* and *you never*, or the use of superlatives like *dumbest, laziest*, and so on, are obvious exaggerations. Whoever's using them is resorting to "poetic" license. You can generally disregard such statements and should definitely avoid using them when dealing with your children.

I also said to consider the source. Some people, for example, are prone to using sarcasm. They can't seem to help themselves. Sarcasm oozes out of every pore, and they are always resorting to that sarcastic tone and manner.

Is the person who is criticizing you a constant complainer and nitpicker? Do his words really carry weight, or can they be dismissed because he never does anything but complain and criticize anyway?

Finally, when you consider the moment, you must realize that all sorts of things are said in the heat of anger that aren't meant and aren't true. And unfortunately, parents say their full share of such "heat-of-the-moment" hurtful and damaging things. In the last chapter we talked about learning to count to ten, and not to speak without thinking first. That's wonderful advice for you—but unfortunately, you're not able to reform *your* parents' ways and help them to stop speaking before they think. If your mother's in her seventies or eighties, for instance, she's pretty well set in her ways, and the best thing you can do is recognize her complaints and criticisms for what they are and learn to live with them.

You'll Never Please Some People

The third item on our list of things you must remember in order to overcome the damage inflicted by critical parents is this: You can't please some people no matter what you do. (So don't spend too much time worrying about vindicating yourself.)

Remember the parable of the father and son who couldn't please people no matter who walked and who rode on the donkey?

Well, a problem for many defeated perfectionists is that they are bound and determined to have people like them. If you look on their backs, you're going to find footprints, because they often take on a very close resemblance to doormats. I'll let Joe or Joan or anyone else walk all over me, because it might make him like me (or because I deserve to be walked on).

The problem, of course, is that it *doesn't* make him like me. It only makes him agree that I'm as worthless as I think I am.

And that's an important point. People will come to see you in the same way you see yourself. If you see yourself as someone who deserves to get pushed around and teased, it won't be too long before other people start pushing you around and teasing you.

If you see yourself as someone who is worthy of respect, you'll be treated with respect . . . for the most part.

But you must remember that it will not be possible for you to get everybody to like you. Not everyone will believe you when you tell the truth. Not everyone will think the story you have written is a good one. Not everyone will think you're good-looking. Not everyone will appreciate your sense of humor . . . and so on and on and on. This is true of your friends, neighbors, business associates, and it's true of your parents. So don't devote your time and energy to proving yourself to others.

I can hear the question now:

"Doesn't it matter what other people think of me?"

Sure it does. Just not that much.

It doesn't matter enough that you should try to shape yourself into what other people expect you to be—or what you think they expect you to be.

This is a particular problem for those who have extremely critical parents. They come to believe that they'll never really *measure up*, and so they often attempt to hide behind a false front. They may tell lies, exaggerate their accomplishments, or hide behind a brash, boasting attitude—all in an attempt to hide their true identity. They are convinced that if you really knew them, you wouldn't like them, and so they tell their biggest lies to themselves.

There is a popular situation comedy called "Perfect Strangers," which centers around the slapstick antics of two cousins, Larry and Balki. Balki is newly arrived in the United States from some mythical European country, while Larry is the native American who knows it all and wants to show his cousin how things are done there.

The only problem is that Larry must have grown up in a home with critical parents. He never seems to be content to be just himself . . . especially when it comes to trying to impress the ladies. The inevitable result, of course, is that Larry often ends up looking like a fool . . . or worse.

On one such episode, after Larry had made himself look like a fool in the eyes of a woman who really liked him, Balki gave him a good bit of advice: "Cousin," he said, "she likes you for what you are . . . but you want her to like you for what you are not."

That's a nice bit of wisdom from a "silly" slapstick sitcom!

And it's something that every product of critical parents ought to remember. Most people will like you if you simply try to be yourself. If they don't like you for yourself, then you're better off without them anyway.

In his documentary-style movie, *Zelig*, Woody Allen portrayed a man who was so afraid to offend anyone that he literally became a human chameleon. When he was in a New Orleans jazz band he became black, when he was in a "fat man's" organization he became fat, and so on. He visited Chinatown and became Chinese, he traveled to Nazi Germany and became a Nazi, and on and on. The man had absolutely no identity of his own but went to ludicrous lengths to be part of whatever group was "in" at the moment.

The movie was funny, but upon reflection it's only a slight exaggeration of the way many people live their lives—afraid to be themselves, afraid to stand up for what they really believe in, content to drift along with the crowd.

This can go so far that the defeated perfectionist doesn't trust his own opinions.

In politics, for instance, he may study all the issues, know the candidates, and then, on that basis, decide how he's going to vote.

But then he discovers that three of his acquaintances are voting for the candidate of the other party. Even though he's done his own research and is basing his vote on his knowledge of the issues involved, he'll let his friends change his opinion. He has such a low opinion of himself that he thinks his friends' opinions are better than his own. And the truth may be that they're basing their votes simply on a hunch, party loyalty, or the color of the candidate's eyes.

I'm only using politics as an example. This attitude can extend into every area of the life of the offspring of critical parents.

It is imperative to remember this advice, and repeat it to yourself every time you're tempted to give in to feelings of worthlessness: "It is impossible to please everyone, and the very best thing I can do is just be myself."

Why Do I Feel the Way I Do?

If you're really going to overcome your feelings of self-doubt, inadequacy, and/or rejection, it's important that you come to understand why you feel the way you do.

And, unless you're actually living the life that Rodney Dangerfield always pretends is his, it's not because you're inferior, helpless, weak, or any of a dozen other lies you may believe about yourself. Your feelings about yourself were drummed into you by others—most likely by your parents.

Once you understand where you picked up these lies about your self-worth, you will be better able to disregard them.

Before going any further, I want to caution you about one thing, and that is that we are not looking for someone to blame. We are not interested in affixing blame or pointing fingers at other people, but rather in helping the defeated perfectionist understand the root of his problem.

Anybody who's ever done much in the way of gardening can tell you that the only way to defeat weeds is to attack them at the root. If you chop the tops off, they'll grow right back, mean and strong as ever. When you pull them out, you've got to pull them out roots and all. That's the way it is with feelings of self-doubt and rejection. We have to see the root—how those wrong feelings were planted in the first place—and then we can get rid of them and get on with life the way it's supposed to be lived.

It may be that you are the product of critical parents and don't even realize it. It's not always obvious.

Lorraine was troubled by a very poor self-image, but insisted that her childhood had been a happy one. She remembered feeling secure and loved and at first wouldn't even consider the idea that her problems may have been partly due to her parents' critical attitude toward her.

The very suggestion made her angry. Why, her folks had done everything any parents could be expected to do for their daughter. There had been piano lessons, ballet lessons, gymnastics, camp in the summer. They had seen to it that she was accepted in one of the finest colleges in the country and had helped her pay her way through it. They had done all of this despite the fact that they were not well-to-do by any means and often had to do without things they wanted in order to give their little girl the things that she wanted.

But when Lorraine really thought about her childhood, a startling pattern began to emerge. Those piano lessons? She hadn't really wanted them, but her mother had wanted them for her. She hadn't really wanted the ballet lessons or the trips to camp in the summer either.

In fact, she hadn't even been sure she wanted to attend college. She had always loved art and was more interested in art school, but her father had always dreamed that his daughter would be a success in the business world—so here she was with a degree in business administration.

Still, Lorraine bristled at the thought that her parents had anything to do with her attitude about herself.

"They only wanted what was best for me," she said.

Unfortunately, they had taken the attitude that they always knew what was "best" for their daughter, and her input was rarely, if ever, considered. When she finally convinced them, after two fruitless years, to allow her to drop the piano lessons, she remembered that, "I knew they were really disappointed in me, but they never let me know it."

My question: If they didn't let her know it, then how *did* she know it? They may not have walked up to her and said,

"Lorraine, we're disappointed in you." But they let her know through sad expressions, sighs, and body language. Those sorts of "unspoken comments" can be at least as harmful as saying outright how you feel. Little Lorraine was receiving the message that, "I've really let Mom and Dad down. They feel so bad about it, but they're too nice to say anything to me."

And so, she was getting a double whammy. She felt bad in the first place because she had been such a disappointment to her parents, and then she felt even worse because they were going to such lengths to "hide" their disappointment from her. Or at least she thought that's what they were doing.

Lorraine also defended her parents by saying that they had pushed her only because they knew that life was tough and only those who pushed themselves to the limit were successful.

Could she remember any occasions when her parents seemed to be satisfied with her performance?

She was sure she could.

"Give me an example."

She couldn't.

So Lorraine eventually came to see that her parents, although definitely low-key and not screamers nor verbal abusers, had always been critical of her. And now that she was grown and on her own, she was carrying on the tradition by being incredibly hard on herself.

That's the way it works for children of critical parents. It's as if the torch of criticism is passed from one generation to the next.

Again, once Lorraine came to see that her lack of self-confidence had been instilled in her by her parents, she was ready to make a new start in life.

She said she'd always heard the old joke about the man who went to the psychiatrist for help in overcoming an inferiority complex. After two or three visits, the doctor said, "You know, you don't have an inferiority complex. You really *are* inferior."

Well, she'd always figured that was her. Other people might have complexes, but her problem was that she really *was* inferior! Bullcrumble! It was a relief for her to see that just about anyone growing up in her family would have developed the same sort of self-doubts.

There are many reasons and many ways parents are critical of their children. They may be critical even because they are jealous of their children. This isn't as uncommon as you would think.

Let's say Dad had to drop out of school after the sixth grade to take care of his family. He'll tell you that he wants his children to do better than he did—but deep down inside he doesn't. He feels that if his children surpass him, they won't be proud of him anymore, and so he does his best to keep them in their place. He may not even realize what he's doing.

Or Mom may have always been shy and plain, not too popular with the boys. Her daughter, on the other hand, is pretty and bright and attracts boys the way a porch light in summer attracts moths. And even though Mom's resentment is buried deep down in her subconscious, it leads her to tease her daughter about her frizzy hair or her big nose. The result may be that the daughter tends to withdraw, or to think that the boys who flirt with her are really only teasing and making fun of her.

She looks in the mirror and she sees what Mom is talking about. Why, yes, isn't that the most gigantic, misshapen nose you've ever seen in your life? Isn't this hair just the pits?

That's how much impact a critical parent can have on his child. It is a big day when the child comes to realize that the problem is not with him, but with his parents.

A critical parent may simply be one who won't let his child do anything around the house.

"No, Johnny, don't worry about that, I'll do it."

"No, Jenny, don't worry about making your bed, Mom will do that for you later."

We've discussed this before, but it's worth repeating that this sort of behavior sends a message to the child:

"I'll do it because you wouldn't do it right!"

And the child begins to develop the attitude that, "I can't do anything right. I'm a real failure."

Do you suffer from self-doubts and feelings of unworthiness? Take a few minutes to sit back and reflect on your childhood. (It just might be that the problem lies with your parents, and not with you at all.)

Cognitive Self-Discipline

So now you've come to realize that you are the product of critical parents. You can almost come to believe that you're not so bad. Almost . . . but not quite.

You also understand that some people, including parents, are natural-born critics. You know that you don't have to believe everything your parents tell you. And you have come to see that you can't spend your life worrying about what everyone else thinks of you. But how do you translate all of that into personal success? What's the next step?

Jesse Jackson's PUSH (People United to Save Humanity) campaign has done a good job of instilling some pride in minority and inner-city students. One of the things he does is have them repeat, "I am somebody! I am somebody!"

The first time his audience may say it sort of halfheartedly, as if they don't really believe it. They're only saying it because he told them to. But the second time it's louder, and the third time they're absolutely shouting it out, "I *AM* somebody!" You can see in their eyes, and hear in their voices, that they believe what they're saying.

Is it so much hype and hocus-pocus? Not on your life. It changes things. You had better believe you're somebody, too. And if you have to look yourself in the mirror every day and say, "I am somebody," well, then do it.

I don't care how often or how much your parents may have criticized (or still criticize) you or put you down. It's like the poster says, "I know I'm somebody special because God doesn't make any junk." You have to keep telling yourself that until you come to know it's true.

This is a part of "cognitive self-discipline." It is coming to know your true self, including your capabilities and your weaknesses. It's coming to understand the experiences and relationships with other people which have shaped you.

But more than this, it is coming to know that there have been built into you tendencies to do or say the very things that will keep you trapped in the cycle of failure and rejection.

A person who is exercising cognitive self-discipline will be able to say, "I can see that my tendency is to act in this direction, but I am going to exercise self-discipline and go in the other direction."

Remember the movie *Star Wars*? In the climactic scene, Luke Skywalker was streaking in to lower the boom on the evil Deathstar. And then he heard the voice of Obi-Wan Kenobi telling him to "trust the force, Luke."

Well, good old Luke flipped off every electronic device in his cockpit and went with the force—which is to say he trusted his feelings. Of course, everyone in the world knows that he blew that Deathstar into so much talcum powder. (Somehow leaving behind enough bad guys for at least two sequels)

Remember that dramatic scene? Good!

Now forget it.

Why? Because if you are a product of critical parents—or for any other reason have tendencies toward being a defeated perfectionist—the last thing in the world you need to do is follow your feelings.

What do those feelings tell you? That you're going to fail, so you might as well not even try. That whatever you attempt, something is going to go wrong, so there's no use in attempting.

Your feelings may tell you that you don't count unless other people notice you and so you go out of your way to get their attention. Or they may drive you to an absolute panic with the idea that you're not doing something right. You're doing the best you can, but you know it's not perfect, and that makes the muscles in your stomach tighten and your shoulders begin to ache as the weight of the world comes down upon you. Those feelings are telling you, "It's got to be perfect, or it's no good at all."

Believe me, if you're ever going to break out of a cycle of disappointment and rejection, you have to realize that you've been following a plan for your life which is nothing but a big lie. (Remember chapter 2? Alfred Adler and the concept of life-style?)

In *Star Wars*, Luke had a hard time deciding to go with his feelings. The truth is that it's vastly more difficult to decide that you have to go *against* your feelings. It takes a tremendous amount of self-discipline, fortitude, and an iron-willed determination to say, "I am going to take control of my life and do what's best for me, even though it may feel as if I'm doing the wrong thing."

Even those little decisions to not follow your feelings will trouble you at first. But once you've had success with those, you'll begin to take charge of your life in other, seemingly more important areas.

For example, let's say that your parents' constant criticisms and nitpicking left you with the desire to have everyone think highly of you. As a result, you're a sucker for every salesman who comes along.

And you keep getting those telephone calls from people wanting to sell you everything from cemetery plots to trips to the Bahamas. In the last year alone, you've had your chimney cleaned three times, had your house inspected for termites twice, and spent a small fortune on tickets to concerts and other events hosted by charities.

Every time you buy something from one of these telephone solicitors, you hang up the phone and wonder, *How in the world did I let him talk me into that?*

Part of the problem is that you're afraid the caller won't like you (and why should you care what he thinks, since you don't even know him?) so you want him to understand why it is that you're not going to give a hundred dollars so his civic group can take ten needy kids to the circus.

"I know it's a good cause," you say, "but our budget is a little tight this month, and—"

"Well, that's okay," he interrupts. "The circus isn't for another two months, so I can send your invoice out today, and you'll still have thirty days to send in your check."

"I don't know. . . . I . . . er . . . that's still a lot of money."

"If that's too much for you, how about fifty dollars? That'll send five kids to the circus, and *anybody* can afford fifty dollars."

He says it with a sarcastic sort of sneer in this voice, and you don't like it at all, but for some reason you hear yourself say, "Oh, yes . . . I suppose we can afford fifty dollars."

There, you've sabotaged your budget and spent money you couldn't afford to spend, all because your sense of self-worth is so dependent upon what others think of you it will not allow you to do anything that might be in the least bit offensive to them!

Don't get me wrong. I'm not picking on charities who want to take needy kids to the circus. That's a wonderful thing. But I also realize that you cannot support each charity that comes along, no matter how worthy it may be.

What did you do wrong?

If you didn't want to buy the tickets, you should have said a polite but firm no. You didn't owe the caller any other information. When you started to explain yourself to him—trying so carefully not to offend him—that's when you lost control of the situation.

If after you had said no, the salesman had been persistent, you could have simply said, "I'm really not interested." And if he wouldn't let up after that you would be perfectly within your rights to hang up on him.

Of course, if you had done that, you'd feel absolutely terrible. Why? Because you had gone against your feelings. Your feelings that tell you to be nice to everybody because the way other people feel about you is the way you feel about yourself.

If you're a really bad case, you probably would have agonized over the situation for several hours, hoping you hadn't hurt the man's feelings too badly.

Believe me, that man makes hundreds of telephone calls during a day, and by the end of that time he wouldn't even remember that you hung up on him.

He won't go home and tell his wife, "Boy, that Mary Wilson—you know, the one who lives at 1123 Magnolia Street—she was really mean to me today."

I'm not advocating that the defeated perfectionist should be selfish. But you have to love yourself enough to express your own point of view, and that includes saying no when you want to say no.

So get tough. Tell yourself that for a week you're going to turn down every salesman who comes your way. And then do it. You don't have to be mean or angry. You can be polite and still say no. Practice with yourself in the mirror if you have to, and don't use words like "I'm sorry" or "I'd like to, but. . . ." A simple, "No, thank you," will suffice.

If you have an inconsiderate neighbor, who exasperates you by always calling you for last-minute favors, learn to say no to her, too. Suppose she wants you to watch her three-year-old twins for a couple of hours while she runs to the beauty parlor, and that this isn't the first time she's imposed on you. Your feelings tell you, "Oh, go ahead, it won't hurt you that much. You don't want to rock the boat."

But my advice to you is that it won't hurt you that much to simply say, "I can't help you right now."

"You can't?"

"No, I can't."

"But . . . why not?"

"I just can't do it."

Again, you don't owe anyone else an explanation for your no. You don't have to make up a story and tell her that you can't do it because you've invited the Millard Fillmore Fan club in for tea. Tell her you can't do it and let it go at that. If she becomes angry it's her problem, not yours. Just remember that she was the one who wanted to impose upon you—not the other way around.

A woman who is the product of critical parents may have feelings that tell her she's nothing at all unless she has a man in her life. So if one dating relationship ends, she'll quickly look for another one. Often, she'll become involved with someone who is not good for her, simply because she can't stand to be without a man.

In this situation, the woman needs to go against her feelings by determining to be by herself for a while—to take time to get to like being alone with herself or with her female friends. She should do this even if it means turning down a few requests for dates.

And a date doesn't have to be turned down in such a way that angers the person doing the asking. There's nothing wrong with saying, "No, I can't. But I hope you'll ask me again." That lets him know that you don't have anything against him, that you'd like to go out with him, but that you can't right now.

Then, in the week or so that she is not dating anyone, Ms. "Got-to-have-a-man-in-my-life" should spend her time reading, painting, enrolling in a dance class, or perhaps going out with female friends. In other words, the time should be filled up with activities, not spent sitting at home thinking about how miserable she is because she doesn't have a steady boyfriend.

At first, getting by without a dating relationship is going to be hard for her. She'll be out with her friends thinking, *What am I doing out with the girls, when I should be in the company of some handsome man?* But in the meantime, she's learning that she doesn't really have to have a man in her life at every moment. She's being set free from the tendency to get involved in unhealthy relationships just for the sake of having a man around. And, she may even have enough fun with her female friends that she begins to believe that she's intelligent, witty, and so on, even when there's not a man around to tell her she is.

Do It Now!

Another common problem for the defeated perfectionist son or daughter of critical parents is the tendency to procrastinate. This isn't a procrastination born out of laziness or forgetfulness, but out of fear. The defeated perfectionist is convinced that he can't do a perfect job, so he won't do any job at all.

Suppose this is your particular problem, and your boss gives you an important report to write. You do your research and get everything together, and then nothing else happens. You're paralyzed by thoughts like, *I know the boss won't like what I do. What if my information is wrong?* And you worry nearly to the point of making yourself sick about the wording you'll use, because you want every single word to be perfect.

Going against your feelings in a case such as this means that you simply make up your mind that you're not going to worry yourself to death—and start writing.

I understand that it won't be that easy, but you can do it if you put your mind to it.

When your feelings say, *The boss may not like it,* tell yourself, *But I'll do the best job I can do.*

When you feel, *My information may be wrong,* remind yourself that you've done your research.

And quit worrying about being another Hemingway. Force yourself to sit down and start writing. If you decide later that you don't like what you've written, you can always revise it. This way you will at least have something to revise.

These are the sorts of things I'm talking about when I say that the defeated perfectionist must learn to go against his feelings.

Look into your life and see the wrong choices you have made; all those decisions that have cost you and brought about rejection and defeat in your life.

Chances are good that you made those decisions because you were following your feelings instead of your brain. But now it's time to make some drastic changes in the way you operate.

Here are a few other suggestions for changing your game plan and improving your life.

1. Give yourself permission to be imperfect. You might as well face the fact that you've never been perfect and you never will be. So give yourself a break. Make a conscious effort to take it easy on yourself—and others, too.

2. Don't be so quick to put yourself down. Allow yourself some freedom. Don't get so bound up now in overcoming your self-defeating actions that you become angry with yourself when you don't say no when you want to, or when you procrastinate, or when you do anything else that falls short of the goals you've set for yourself.

If you've just bought another set of everlasting light bulbs from a salesman, and you already have a closet full of everlasting light bulbs, don't berate yourself about it. Shrug it off, try to develop a sense of humor about it, and promise yourself that you'll do better next time.

It's going to take you some time to change patterns that have been ingrained in you since childhood. Realize this, and know that time is on your side.

At the end of each day, look back over what you've done, and see where you could have acted in ways that would have been better for you. But again, don't do it in the sense of "Wow, I've really goofed up again." Do it with the attitude of learning from your mistakes and realize that a review of this type can be a big step toward a better day tomorrow.

3. Do something nice for yourself. Remember the TV commercial where the woman tells you that the product she's just bought cost a little bit more than the other brands? But then she says, "But that's okay . . . I'm worth it."

You have to start thinking like that woman. No, I'm not advocating that you go around thinking that you're better than everyone else, and so you should always have the best of everything. But I'm saying that you should give yourself a treat once in a while, because you're worth it.

Most defeated perfectionists have a hard time being nice to themselves. They'll want prime rib but they'll order chicken because they don't want to be extravagant. Even when they do indulge and buy a much-needed dress, suit, or what-have-you, they'll wrestle with their consciences for hours afterward.

"Oh, I don't think I should have bought this. Maybe I should take it back. After all . . . I have other dresses in my closet. And I could have found one that wasn't so expensive."

Well, you've got to stop that kind of thinking right now! You deserve some pleasure in this life, just as you deserve to succeed and not to fail.

4. Learn to think positively. Try to get rid of pessimistic attitudes. Learn to see the glass as half full instead of half empty. Positive thinking is a powerful force, and I urge you to use it. There's nothing magic about it, but seeing things in a positive light—including yourself—will give you the attitude needed to succeed. If you go into something thinking you're going to fail, chances are good that you will fail. But if you can have a positive attitude, you will approach the task at hand in a more relaxed and confident manner, and you'll do a better job.

You can develop such a positive attitude by thinking about the good things that have happened to you recently. Think about your good friends and how much they mean to you.

5. Learn to be forgiving. Don't hold a grudge, whether it's against your wife or husband, your mother or father, your child, or even yourself.

Everybody makes mistakes, and just about everybody is going to let you down at one time or another.

You need to realize that making mistakes has been a part of human nature ever since Adam and Eve came upon the scene, and you're not about to change that. Expecting your friends and relatives to be infallible is expecting too much, and it will get you into trouble.

In fact, I suggest that you stop right now. If you're holding a grudge against someone, for whatever reason, make a conscious effort to forgive them. Ask God to help you. If it's a friend (or a former friend) call him and tell him that you want to make things right between you. If you're angry with yourself for something you've done, look at yourself in the mirror and forgive yourself! It may sound silly, but it can be effective. Just remember that forgiveness is hard to find without God's help.

If you are a product of critical parents, make an effort to forgive them, too. Yes, they may have got you started along the path of rejection and failure, but there's no need to stay on that path. You need to put all of that behind you, and that means you must learn to forgive.

So . . . once again . . . if you want to change the way your life is turning out, you must learn to be gentler with yourself—and with others, learn the art of positive thinking, and practice forgiveness.

And it is always helpful to step back and take a look at your life in an effort to see what you might be doing that brings about failure and rejection.

Ask yourself, *Is there anything I could be doing differently that would help to change things for me?* Be honest with yourself. And if you see that the answer is, *Yes, I could make some changes,* then go ahead and make them.

5

The Problem with Guilt

The human conscience is an amazing thing. Some people have far too much, some have far too little, and some seem to have none at all. (How else can you explain monsters such as Adolf Hitler, Josef Stalin, and, closer to our day, the murderous Saddam Hussein?)

"Whoa," you say, "back up a minute, Dr. Leman. I understand what you're saying about Hitler and Stalin, and about other folks who seem to be lacking something in the way of a conscience. But did I read the first part of that sentence correctly? Did you actually say that some people have too much in the way of conscience?"

I sure did.

"Would you take a minute and explain that, please?"

Gladly.

The person who is a defeated perfectionist generally has a conscience that's way too big. So big, in fact, that it magnifies shortcomings and failures and won't let its owner forget sins or imaginary sins of years ago, even though they have long since been repented of or paid for.

Your conscience is a wonderful gift from the Creator, and it's doing what it's designed to do if it keeps you from stealing, cheating on your income tax, chasing your neighbor's spouse, beating your children, or any other similar activity.

But if it keeps whispering to you that you're the lowest of the low, simply because you failed an algebra course in school ten years ago or because you don't spend enough time emailing your mother, then it's overdoing it a bit.

Don't get me wrong. If you flunk an algebra course, I don't think you should just shrug it off and say, "So what?" And, if you don't email your mother very often, it's good that you should realize that and make up your mind to do better. But if things such as that are keeping you awake at night or have you terribly depressed, then something's wrong.

In the last chapter I talked a little bit about forgiveness and how important it is to be forgiving. Sometimes the hardest person for me to forgive is myself. That's especially true if I am living the rejected, failed life-style of defeated perfectionists. They can be what I would call "Gluttons of Guilt." They can never get enough of putting themselves down, beating their breasts, and wishing they could be like somebody else—nearly anybody else! Often, such a person can easily tolerate in others what he can't stand in himself.

If Barbara is talkative and monopolizes the conversation, she's being friendly and outgoing. If I do it, I'm talking too much and boring everyone, so why can't I ever learn to keep my mouth shut?

If Lawrence didn't finish that important report in time, well, he's been awfully busy, and everybody misses a deadline once in a while. If I do the same thing, it's another proof of my incompetency, and it's probably what everyone expected.

And on it goes.

Now, it doesn't always work like that. These Gluttons of Guilt are often just as critical of everyone else as they are of themselves.

Or, in some instances, more critical. But when that happens, most often it's because of misdirected self-hatred. It's kind of hard for me to abuse myself verbally, so I'll take it out on you.

After all, I'm not exactly going to hurt my feelings if I lash out at myself and call me names. (I wouldn't take myself seriously anyway, because I know what a bozo I am.) So, to express the way I feel about myself, I'll lash out at someone else. Like you, for instance.

Either way, the situation is brought about by an overly developed conscience and a tendency to gather and hang on to guilt. And guilt is never a good thing to hang on to, whether it's my own or someone else's.

I think of Marianne, whose husband had discovered that she was having an affair, some fifteen years ago.

"I don't know how or why it happened," she sobbed. "I was bored, and we were having some problems, and I just needed someone to talk to." She found a terrific listener in a co-worker who soon turned into much more than that.

When her husband discovered what was going on, he thought about filing for a divorce but decided he loved his wife too much and was willing to give her a second chance. Marianne promised that she'd end the affair immediately, which she did.

So for the last fifteen years she had been as good a wife as she knew how to be. She wanted so badly to make up for what she had done that she began to cater to her husband's every whim . . . and he had hundreds of them. If he wanted breakfast in bed, she brought it. When it came time to plan the vacation trip, her input was ignored. They did whatever he wanted to do, whenever he wanted to do it, and Marianne slowly became more of a servant than a wife.

The problem was that neither she nor her husband would truly forgive and forget.

How many times during these fifteen years had her husband reminded her of her mistake? Marianne wasn't sure, but it had been plenty. Just about every time she wanted to stand up for herself, to insist on being treated as an equal partner in the marriage, he would start talking about the terrible thing she had done.

As for Marianne, she didn't have to listen to that, but she always did. After all, she was carrying around enough guilt to choke an elephant, so she felt that she deserved whatever disrespect her husband wanted to show her.

It was apparent that he was actually enjoying being the offended party. He was getting a tremendous amount of mileage out of this thing.

And Marianne, even though she hated being picked at and put down, was submitting to it because the ill treatment was a way of doing penance, of paying for her mistake.

By this time, her problem went much deeper than just her relationship with her husband. His constant references to her affair, his putdowns, and his refusal to take her seriously as his equal in the marriage had affected other areas of her life.

She had come to the point where she was afraid to make decisions. She would stand in an aisle at the supermarket for ten minutes trying to decide between two brands of soup, and as soon as she made up her mind she knew somehow that she was making the wrong choice. She was insecure and tongue-tied in front of people, figuring that they could sense her worthlessness and didn't want to hear anything she had to say anyway. And she was unable to effectively discipline her children because they could easily convince her that she was wrong and they were right.

For instance, eleven-year-old Tommy would come home with his pockets full of metal slugs he had picked up where the new subdivision was being built—a place his mother had told him to stay away from.

"Tommy, you know I don't want you going over there."

"But I told you I was going over there, and you said it was okay."

"I don't remember telling you—"

"Sure you did, Mom. Don't you remember? You were standing right there, and I came in with Bobby, and asked you if we could go to the construction site, and you said, 'Sure.'"

Now Marianne didn't remember any such conversation. In fact she was 99 percent certain it had never taken place. But her own insecurities wouldn't let her stick to her guns, and she would always end up giving in.

"Oh . . . well . . . I guess if you asked me. But I don't want you going over there anymore."

"Sure, Mom." Of course, Tommy never meant his "Sure, Mom," because he knew how easily he could manipulate her and get her to give in. Her daughter Joanne was the same, and both kids knew they could get away with murder because Mom would never really be able to discipline them. Besides, if she tried, Dad would usually be on their side, and not hers.

The doubts and self-guilt she felt had come to affect every area of her life.

What was the answer for Marianne? First of all, she needed to truly forgive herself for what she had done. She needed to realize that she wasn't the only human being who had ever made such a mistake and, furthermore, that it wasn't entirely her fault. I'm not saying that she needed to look for excuses for her behavior, such as blaming the whole thing on the man who "seduced" her, or on her "uncaring" husband who had sent her into the arms of another man. But what I am saying is that she needed to really look back over the event from the vantage point of fifteen years later and, as much as was possible, without looking through the distorting filter of emotion, analyze what had really happened.

Many factors entered into Marianne's infidelity. None of these excused her behavior, but they all had to be taken into account if Marianne was ever going to free herself from her self-flagellation as an "unworthy" woman, deserving only of being overlooked and disregarded. She needed to have a proper unemotional evaluation of what happened and why, seeing her own guilt, yes, but not pinning the blame for the entire incident upon her own shoulders.

Once she had done that, she needed to make a conscious and conscientious effort to forgive herself.

I talked in the last chapter about looking into the mirror and verbally forgiving yourself. If that's what it would take for Marianne to put this behind her, that's exactly what she needed to do. And after that, even when she didn't really feel like it, she was to act as if she had been forgiven.

The next time her husband tried to bring up the ancient past, she was to say: "That happened fifteen years ago. I'm sorry that it ever happened, but it's over and done with. I've forgiven myself for that, and I don't want you to bring it up again."

Naturally, her husband wasn't going to like that, and there was no telling how he would react. But that didn't really matter. Marianne had to stick to her guns. She had forgiven herself, and she now expected her husband to follow through and do the same. When he continued to put her down and make demands on her, her gut reaction would be to do what she had always done . . . namely, give in and go along with him. But this time she was to go against her feelings.

She was to insist upon being listened to in other aspects of their life together, too. She wanted to be considered when vacation plans were being made, to have control of the television from time to time, or decide what movie the family was going to see—all those things that any wife and mother should be a part of, but which she had been denied for so long because of her guilt.

Forgiving herself wasn't that easy, but once she had made the decision to do it, she stood by it. She wanted her husband's forgiveness, but if he wasn't willing to give it after she had proved herself to be a faithful and supportive wife and a proper mother for fifteen years . . . well, the problem was his and not hers. She hoped he would choose to truly put the past behind him, but if he chose not to do so, she wasn't going to let it keep her bound up for the rest of her life.

Having been set free in her relationship with herself, and with her husband, she became more forceful in other areas of her life. She followed the advice that says, "Act as if you believe you're somebody important, and other people will think so, too."

Once again, she had to go against her feelings. When she felt like caving in to her children, she didn't. When discipline was needed, she administered it—and wouldn't be talked out of it.

She often felt like she was a walking, talking dish of gelatin, but made sure that nobody else knew that. And, you know what? It worked. She stopped carrying three hundred pounds of guilt on her shoulders, she stopped letting anyone and everyone push her around, and her life changed dramatically for the better.

Even her husband was able, finally, to put the past behind him. He hasn't brought it up in months and when he and Marianne get into an argument—as husbands and wives always will—it is at least a fair fight, with nobody dredging up old hurts from a long-dead past.

Accepting God's Forgiveness

Marianne's longtime inability to forgive herself was really nothing new. People have been punishing themselves for their misdeeds, real and imagined, for centuries.

The ancient Roman statesman Cato put it this way: "I can pardon everyone's mistakes but my own."[1] He surely spoke for thousands who have lived both before and after him.

But as for Marianne, now that she had come face to face with the problem of unresolved guilt, she also was finally able to accept something else she had always acknowledged in her head, but never really believed with her heart: That God had also forgiven her.

As a Christian, she knew that her behavior had been sinful. She also knew what the Bible taught, that if she repented of any sin, no matter what it was, and asked the Lord to forgive her, He would certainly do it.

"I've probably asked God at least a hundred times to forgive me," she had said. "And I'll feel better for a while, but then it comes back to me, and I have to ask Him all over again."

Accepting God's forgiveness can be a particularly difficult problem for the defeated perfectionist who is bound up in his own guilt and failure.

But guilt serves a purpose. It shows us when we've done something wrong, so that we might change our ways and not make the same mistake again. But guilt that doesn't do anything but bring a person under condemnation and make him wallow in his own worthlessness is self-destructive. If you don't deal with that kind of guilt, it will kill you.

If you've done somebody wrong, ask for their forgiveness. If they're willing to forgive you, you've gained a friend. If they're not willing to forgive you, realize that you have at least done what was required of you, and then forgive yourself.

If you have done something that you feel requires God's forgiveness, tell Him about it and ask Him to forgive you. Then read those Scripture verses over and over until you can honestly accept the forgiveness He offers.

One young man told me he was so burdened with guilt that he prayed nearly every day, asking God to please forgive the things he had done. And even though he knew what the Bible had to say, he still had a terrible time accepting God's forgiveness.

"I used to get out of bed during the middle of the night," he said, "and slip into the bathroom. I'd kneel down there, in front of the toilet, and ask Him to please, please forgive me.

"I'd sit there in the dark for a while, waiting for something to happen, only nothing ever did." After a few minutes, he'd dejectedly tiptoe back into the bedroom, being careful not to wake up his wife, who was sleeping peacefully.

Finally, one night, something happened.

"It was as if I heard God's voice, although, of course, I didn't really hear anything," he explained. "But I sensed deep down that a voice was saying, 'Why do you keep asking Me to forgive you, when I forgave you the first time you asked?'"

Upon that realization, a sense of peace and joy washed over him and he was set free. Now, your freedom from guilt may not come as his did, like a voice in the middle of the night. But the voice of the Lord speaks to all who are bound up in that same way, saying the same thing: "Why do you keep asking Me to forgive you, when I forgave you the first time you asked?"

Why indeed? Why is it so hard for some people to accept God's forgiveness?

The primary reason, I believe, is because our relationship with God is patterned after our relationship with our earthly father.

If your father was harsh, judgmental, and unforgiving, you are probably going to see your heavenly Father in those terms. If your dad wasn't around much and didn't seem to care what you did so long as you kept out of his hair, you're going to believe that God isn't really all that interested in you either.

And when it comes to carrying around a truckload of guilt, that's a characteristic that's usually built into you by your family. Often this starts during the adolescent years, when people tend to be awkward and feel guilty about nearly everything anyway.

In Marianne's case, her guilt came from her sense of having done her husband wrong, but the tendency to be a Glutton of Guilt had been there long before her marriage and its subsequent failure.

An overactive conscience is not something you inherit in the same way you inherit blue eyes or red hair or the tendency to be tall and thin. But it is often passed along from generation to generation just the same.

Everyone knows we have had an epidemic of suicide among our nation's teenagers. Suicide, in fact, is the second-leading cause of death among American young people, topped only by automobile accidents.[2] Many theories have been put forward as

131

to why so many of our young people are taking their own lives. It's been suggested that they are afraid to face the future with the threat of global annihilation from nuclear war hanging in front of them. Others say it's because today's youths are growing up disillusioned and rudderless—they don't have a cause to believe in and therefore come to believe that life isn't worth living. Then there are those who blame certain rock music for glamorizing death, suicide in particular. Some pin the blame on drugs or alcohol, and still others on involvement in occult practices.

While I'm certain that all of these things have played a role in the spiraling rate of teen suicides, they don't take into account what I believe to be the major cause of such tragedies, and that is simply an unhealthy home life.

Too many teens and preteens are growing up in homes where they're pushed beyond their limits. They have critical parents who don't seem to know how to do anything but complain and criticize their kids. They're pushed, pushed, pushed beyond their abilities to succeed. And then millions of latch-key children come home every day to empty houses because both parents have to work to make ends meet. That might not be so bad if their parents had time for them during the evenings and weekends, but after Mom and Dad have worked all day, they're often too tired to expend any energy on their children. They want the rest of the time for themselves.

Many of our children are riddled with feelings of guilt. They're guilty because they can't live up to their parents' expectations or because they feel that they are a burden and a bother to their parents. No wonder so many of them are literally drowning in an ocean of guilt!

It would be a wonderful thing if American parents en masse would reevaluate their relationships with their children. Things would improve tremendously if all parents would quit making unreasonable demands on their children or being overly critical of them when they fail. Instead, as we discussed earlier, children should be allowed the freedom to fail. Smart parents will allow their children to develop a sense of self-respect by utilizing reality discipline and letting them be responsible for their own actions. Parents who do not become overly upset about their children's failures and who are not always rushing to the rescue are teaching their children that occasional failures are normal, that to fail in one particular endeavor is not the same as failing at life in general, and that, yes, failure sometimes brings unpleasant consequences, but they can be overcome. The child who is berated for his failures, or whose parents always rush in for the rescue, eventually becomes riddled with guilt. He believes two lies about himself:

1. I *always* do the wrong thing.
2. I'd *never* be able to make it if I didn't have someone close at hand to pull me through.

Guilt is a strange animal. It reproduces faster than rabbits, and it's harder to get rid of than cockroaches!

Look at one of the ways guilt reproduces itself: A woman in a middle-class neighborhood is bothered because the other residents seem to have nicer cars and furniture. Perhaps they wear nicer clothes. And she notices something else, too. In the mornings, when she's sending her husband off to work and her children off to school, the other women in the neighborhood are going off to work, too. Why, she must be the only wife in the entire neighborhood who doesn't work outside the home.

This makes her feel guilty, because perhaps if she were work- ing, her family could have a nicer car, nicer furniture, and nicer clothes. Why, just look at how the neighbors' kids dress. Their little girl always looks so cute in her designer dresses, designer jumpers, or designer jeans. And she knows her own son would be thrilled to have more of those shirts and pants from that expensive surf shop.

So she lets that guilt eat at her for a while, figuring it's her fault that her family doesn't have all of these wonderful things, and then finally decides that she will go to work. Notice that she doesn't go to work because she wants to or even because the family really needs her to. She goes to work purely out of guilt.

How do the kids react? Most likely, they aren't too happy to see Mom going to work. They enjoyed having her there when they came home from school, and it takes some adjustment to come home to an empty house. Beyond that, they probably tend to feel guilty because they realize she went to work to help buy their clothes or pay for their braces or doctor bills or what have you.

If Mom comes home from work in a bad mood, because she really would rather stay home, that compounds the situation. Mom is resentful that she "has" to work, and now she feels guilty because she knows she's irritable and cranky. Wait a minute! I thought she went to work because she was feeling guilty. Now that she's working, she still feels guilty, only for another reason. I thought she was going to work so she could help out, and especially to give the kids the things they wanted. But are they happier now? Not on your life.

And so the merry-go-round of guilt spins round and round.

Guilt is a terrible taskmaster, a self-fulfilling prophecy—a rejection that comes from within and not from without. And I'll tell you something, you'd be money ahead to take a baseball bat and whack yourself in the teeth. It wouldn't hurt half as much, and you'd be over it quicker!

There are several common mistakes Gluttons of Guilt make:

1. They pile one infraction on top of another.
2. They let their children manipulate them.
3. They take the blame when others are responsible.
4. They give in to depression.
5. They believe they deserve to suffer.
6. They judge themselves by what others think of them.
7. They would rather suffer than take steps to change things.[3]

Let's take a closer look at each of these mistakes:

1. They pile one infraction on top of another. Every time one of these discouraged, self-rejected people fails, he runs through his entire list of the other times he has failed.

For instance, suppose Mrs. Guilty is thirty-five pounds over-weight and has a high school reunion coming up. She's determined to get rid of that excess weight and recapture that youthful figure that had the boys' heads turning twenty years ago. She's doing pretty well on her diet until, one day in the mall, she happens to pick up the wonderful aroma of that new cinnamon roll place.

Mmmmm! They smell so good! And she's always loved cinnamon rolls.

Some fifteen minutes later, she sits forlornly at one of those little tables and wonders how she could have done this. Three of those things in one sitting! How many calories are in those things, anyway? Probably fifty thousand apiece! There goes the size eight, the reunion, and, she thinks, her life.

I don't know why I do things like this, she thinks. *I always blow it.* And she looks at the instant replays of all the times she has failed to stick to her diet. Of course, with every scene, she gets deeper into guilt and self-condemnation and more depressed.

If she's really good at this guilt thing, she'll take things well beyond her failed diet and her need to lose some weight. She'll start thinking, *Well it's not only the weight. It's my hair, too. Whatever happened to my hair—it used to be so nice. And my skin. Gosh, why can't I do something about my skin?* She finds a dozen things wrong with her appearance—and blames herself for most of them.

What a pathetic sight! Sitting there in the mall feeling sadder and uglier by the moment!

There are other ways one infraction is piled on top of another. Consider Jeff, who is fairly active in his church and never misses a Sunday.

Then one day, he simply doesn't go. He has no reason for missing, just that it's a rainy Sunday morning, one of those days that seem to beg you to sleep in, and that's what he does.

Afterward, he feels guilty, but he prays about it and figures that the Lord understands. But the following Sunday morning as he's getting dressed for church he starts thinking: *What will I say if anyone asks me where I was last Sunday? I don't really have an excuse for missing.* He suddenly begins to feel as if all eyes will be upon him, and he can hear the people whisper, "Where in the world was Jeff last Sunday? I'll bet he just slept in."

He sits down on the edge of his bed and tries to think of what to do. Finally, he decides not to do anything. He can't face up to people's questions so he decides not to go this week either. And now that he's missed two weeks in a row, he's really in a dilemma. I mean, he might have been able to explain one absence, but two . . . and now three . . . and then four?

It's not long before Jeff feels as if he'll never be able to return to that little church, which he really loved. And he lives in fear that the pastor or one of the deacons will call to ask him what happened, and he won't have the slightest idea what to say. You can see how guilt grows exponentially, like compound interest.

2. They let their children manipulate them. Remember Marianne, and how her children would manipulate and abuse her? This is a common occurrence for parents who are wrapped up in guilt.

In my book *The Pleasers* I gave the example of little Suzy who has been up for three nights in a row watching TV shows, and who, ten minutes before bedtime on the fourth night, announces that she has a book report due in the morning and wants Mom to help her.

Well, quite naturally, Mom is a bit angry. Here Suzy's known about the report all week and hasn't done a thing! Now, at the last moment, she asks for Mom's help.

When Mom says "No," what does Suzy do? She throws it back in Mom's face:

"I knew you wouldn't help me," she says. "And now I'm gonna fail. You never help me!"

If the child is a first-class manipulator, she'll even bring dear old Dad into the equation:

"Dad told me you wouldn't help me!"

What Mom ought to do is ignore Suzy's accusations and her anger and make her go to bed on schedule. If she gets a bad grade, well, that's all a part of reality discipline. But if Mom is controlled by her guilt—if she hears those little voices that say, "Good mothers always help their children"—she'll undoubtedly give in, and she and little Suzy will be up well past both their bedtimes trying to get the book report written.

3. They take the blame when others are responsible. Talk about being in a no-win situation. That happens all the time to the guilt-ridden defeated perfectionist.

Most of the time it's because they have so many "guilt buttons," which are easily pushed, and the people closest to them know so well how to push them.

Karla, for instance, feels that she's a failure as a wife. She can't seem to do anything right, and it's always her fault. She doesn't see that she's being forced into a no-win situation by her husband, Brian.

Tuesday night Brian comes home from work half an hour later than usual. He storms in to the house in an obvious bad mood, saying that he was stuck in the worst traffic jam of the last thirty years. (And maybe he was, maybe he wasn't.)

Karla does her best to make him feel better. She hugs and kisses him and tries to be her cheeriest, even though the dinner she worked so hard on is now cold.

But Brian isn't having any of it:

"What?" he fumes, "My dinner is cold? Great—I have a crummy day at work, I get stuck in a traffic jam, and now I've gotta eat this stuff?"

He spends the rest of the evening pouting and treating Karla as if everything that happened to him were her fault.

Any truly objective analysis of this situation would tell you that both Karla and Brian have a right to be in less than delightful moods. Karla because her husband has come home thirty minutes later than usual and the dinner she worked so hard on is cold. Brian because he had a hard day at work, and followed that up by being trapped in a traffic jam.

But because Karla is one of those who is always willing to take the blame and let others manipulate her, she quietly tiptoes around her man for the rest of the evening, feeling guilty and trying her best to bring him out of his foul mood.

Poor Karla. And the saga doesn't end there.

Wednesday night, Brian comes home right on time, only this time, his wife has delayed dinner for thirty minutes in order to prevent an instant replay of the previous evening's performance.

Nice try, Karla, but it's not going to work. This time Brian is going to be angry because his dinner isn't ready.

"You know I like to eat as soon as I get home!" he'll whine. "Now I won't be able to watch the news after dinner."

Once again, his poor wife feels guilty, even though she hasn't done anything wrong. In fact, the only thing she is really guilty of is going overboard in trying to please her complaining husband. (But the only way she could have pleased him was to be a mind reader or a magician.)

Brian is lucky, of course, that he's married to one of the "guilty" ones. If he wasn't, he'd be more than likely to find himself with a few knuckle bumps on his head! No self-assured woman is going to take that sort of treatment.

But those who are Gluttons of Guilt are constantly put in no-win situations by their husbands, wives, parents, children, bosses, and so on. They are the quickest apologizers around, always willing to take the blame and say, "It's all my fault," even if they really didn't have anything to do with the situation.

Are you always the first one to apologize? Do you often let people put you in no-win situations? If so, welcome to Guilt Gatherers Anonymous.

4. They give in to depression. Depression is a sinister, life-sapping force. If you give in to it the least little bit, it will fasten itself upon you with more tenacity than a snapping turtle. (And the folks in the Tennessee hills always used to say that once a snapping turtle had ahold of you, he wouldn't let go until it thundered. Only it takes more than thunder to get free from depression.)

Just about everyone feels depressed at some time or another, although obviously some people have a much harder time dealing with it than others. The person who is filled with self-doubt and a sense of his own guilt is much more likely to give in to it.

He's depressed and doesn't feel like getting out of bed. So he won't get out of bed. He'll stay there, hiding from the world, not realizing that he's doing the worst thing he could do.

Several times I've mentioned the necessity of going against your feelings, and that's exactly what you have to do when it comes to depression.

The depressed person wants to stay in bed, but what he really needs to do is screw up every bit of strength and courage, get up, and go about his normal routine.

The guilty person can have a hard time with depression, but he has a much easier time talking himself out of feeling good.

"Wait a minute," he'll say, "why am I feeling so good today? I mean, I don't really have anything to feel good about. I've got that report due at work, and I have to buy a new tire for the car, and my lawn needs to be mowed." And on and on. It won't take a whole lot of effort for him to talk himself into a really black mood, which feels more normal to him.

5. They believe they deserve to suffer. When anything bad happens to him, the guilty defeated perfectionist knows exactly why: It's because he's a bad person and deserves exactly what he's getting.

For years, Harry has kept all his extra money in a savings account. The return is not spectacular, but it's steady. Only friends of his keep telling him that he ought to be playing the stock market. There's one stock in particular they've been investing in, and it's done very nicely for them.

Finally, Harry gives in. He takes five thousand dollars from his savings and plunges into the market. For the first few weeks, everything looks great. The stock is moving up every day, and this looks like one of the smartest financial moves he's ever made.

Then, without warning, the bottom falls out of the market. Harry's stock drops twenty dollars a share overnight.

He may be able to outwardly joke about the situation and say, "I don't know why this sort of thing always happens to me." But inwardly he thinks, *I should have known this would happen. I always get just what I deserve.* Somehow, somewhere, Harry feels as if there are very exacting standards that measure the worth of human beings. As he looks back over his life, he sees dozens of places where he goofed up, let others down, or committed outright sins, and he knows that he could never be the person he was meant to be.

Because he is not able to measure up, it is natural to expect that bad things will happen to him. Whatever bad comes his way, from a stubbed toe to a loss in the stock market to a serious illness, Harry will feel that he's getting what he deserves because he's a bad person.

Unfortunately, Harry's feelings about himself may be self-fulfilling. He may expect accidents to happen to him, for instance, so he becomes careless and inattentive.

In his book *Feeling Good,* Dr. David Burns talks about the need to differentiate between healthy regret or remorse—what we might call "Godly" sorrow—and an unhealthy guilt trip.

When you do something that you know you shouldn't have done, it's natural to feel sorry about it, and this is healthy. But it's a giant leap from regretting an action to concluding that, "I'm really a terrible person."

Dr. Burns explains that, ". . . remorse or regret are aimed at behavior, whereas guilt is targeted toward the 'self.'"[4]

6. They judge themselves by what others think of them. Very often, the "guilty" one lives by everyone else's rules. He gets to the point where he doesn't even know what he thinks until someone else tells him.

If one of these people were an artist, she wouldn't have the slightest idea if the painting she just finished was a masterpiece or a piece of junk.

She'd be standing there looking at the painting wondering about it until someone else came along. Then, if he said something like, "Oh, that's a mess. The colors are all wrong and the perspective is terrible," she'd believe it. She would see all those flaws clearly, even if they weren't really there.

Very often, this is how the guilty ones live their lives, trying as hard as they can to measure up to someone else's expectations. This is especially difficult if the persons whose standards they are trying to meet are arbitrary and capricious. (Remember Karla trying to adjust dinner to Brian's unpredictable schedule and desires.)

7. They would rather suffer than take steps to change things. It's not always easy to change. It may not be easy to go around carrying a load of guilt, but if it's the way you've always lived your life, and it comes naturally to you—well, at least it's a comfortable type of pain.

Sometimes it's easier to keep on living by the same old rules, no matter how harsh they might be, than to break out and begin living in freedom.

The Glutton of Guilt can be like the man who's been in prison for twenty years. In two weeks he will have served his time and he'll be free to go. Only he doesn't *want* to go. He's become so used to life behind bars that he can't imagine what it would be like to live on the outside. In prison, he at least knows that every day will be the same, he knows where he's going to stay, what he's going to have for lunch and dinner, and so on. The outside world looks uncertain, and dangerous.

The biggest step for any person whose life is controlled by guilt is to make the decision that he really is tired of living this way, and that he really *does* want to change. Unless you have that desire, things are never going to change.

Once you've decided that you are going to change and stop living the guilty life, there are several steps you need to make:

1. Quit holding on to guilt.
2. Don't feel guilty, don't take the blame, and don't apologize when it really isn't your fault.
3. Don't let people push your guilt buttons.
4. Lower your high-jump bar of life.
5. Stop living by the other person's agenda.
6. Stop kicking yourself around.
7. Learn to "call an audible" at the scrimmage line.[5]

Once again, let's go over these steps to overcoming guilt one at a time.

1. Quit holding onto guilt. How do you do this? By learning to forgive yourself, and others, too.

If you feel that you have truly wronged someone, go to that person and seek his forgiveness. If you feel that someone has wronged you, make an attempt to reestablish that relationship.

You don't want to call someone you haven't spoken to in years and say something like, "You know, you really did me dirty back five years ago, but I'm calling to let you know I forgive you." That's not the best attitude in the world, and the reaction you'd get would likely be something such as, "What do you mean, you forgive me? I never did anything to you."

Instead, you might say something along the lines of, "I was just thinking about you and wondered how you were doing. Thought I'd give you a call (or drop you a line)." It could be that the other person doesn't want to restore the friendship, and that he enjoys nursing his grudge against you. But you don't have to live your life on his level.

As I mentioned before, if you feel that you have sinned against God, it's important that you seek His forgiveness, too. But remember that there are many Scriptures that speak of His willingness to forgive. If you sincerely asked Him for His forgiveness, you received it.

In his book *Goodbye to Guilt*, Dr. Gerald G. Jampolsky lists six things that holding on to guilt is guaranteed to do:

- Make us feel under attack.
- Justify our feelings of anger toward yourself or someone else.
- Destroy our self-esteem and confidence.
- Make us feel depressed, hollow, and empty.
- Destroy our sense of peace.
- Make us feel unloved.[6]

His steps to overcoming guilt include: Letting go of guilt and not projecting guilt onto others; forgiving and letting go of the past, staying in the present and living in the joy of now; not making demands on anyone, and resisting the temptation to judge.[7]

2. Don't feel guilty, don't take the blame, and don't apologize when it really isn't your fault. I know . . . this is easier said than done. But listen to yourself. Is "I'm sorry" your most commonly used expression?

Resist the temptation to say it.

Let's say your family is going out for dinner and you suggest the local pizza palace. Well, tonight, for some reason, the service is excruciatingly slow. You sit there at the table waiting and waiting, and you know everyone's hungry.

"I'm really sorry," you say. "I can't imagine why it's taking so long. I really feel badly about this."

Why in the world should you apologize? It's not your fault that service is so slow. Now if the pizza came, and you accidentally dropped it on the floor or spilled your drink all over it, then you might have legitimate reason to apologize. But try, try, try not to apologize or take the blame for things over which you have no control.

How many times a day do you say, "I'm sorry"? Do you say you're sorry when other people bump into you? If you walk into an inanimate object, do you immediately, without thinking, apologize?

Now there's nothing wrong with being polite, but that's ridiculous! Cut it out!

3. Don't let people push your guilt buttons. If you are easily manipulated by guilt, don't believe for a minute you're the only one who knows that. Your spouse knows it, your children probably know it, your colleagues at work know it, and your neighbors know it. And, when it suits their purposes to do so, they're not above pushing those guilt buttons.

"Listen, Harriet, I don't know what to do. The boss wants me to get these files finished by tomorrow morning, but I have a really important date tonight." She stands there looking at you with a pathetic look on her face.

She knows what will get you.

"This guy's so special. I think he . . . well . . . he could be the one, and I'd hate to lose the chance to find out."

Jeanine is your closest friend at work, and she knows how guilty you feel every night, watching her go home to her lonely apartment, while you have a loving husband and two perfect children waiting for you.

She's doing a masterful job of pushing those guilt buttons.

"Oh, listen, Jeanine," you say, "I don't really have any big plans for the evening. Why don't you let me do those reports for you?"

"Do you mean it?"

"Sure I'd be glad to."

Well, you'll do it, but that last part wasn't exactly the truth. You're not "glad" to do it at all. It's strictly a matter of guilt, and the truth is that this was the first free evening you'd had in weeks, and one you were really looking forward to. But, somehow, you feel that if you don't help her out Jeanine will never meet Mr. Right and she'll be single, and miserably lonely, for the rest of her life. Which, of course, will be all your fault.

What should you have done? If you really didn't mind doing the work for your friend, fine. But the choice should be based on how you feel and what you want to do—not upon your sense of guilt. Personally, I would resent being manipulated in that way. If Jeanine wanted you to do her work for you, she should have asked you straight out.

Children will attempt to push your guilt buttons in a variety of ways: "But, Mom, all the other girls are allowed to go!" "But, Dad, all the other kids get a lot more allowance than me!" "Mom, can't you please take me to school in the morning, because I have all these books to carry."

If you take your kids at face value, you'll be tempted to think that all the other parents in your neighborhood must have stepped right out of the "Father Knows Best" TV show, while the two of you are a couple of neanderthals who couldn't win a Worst Parents of the Year contest.

Married couples are also usually quite adept at pushing each other's guilt buttons, primarily because they know each other so well.

In some instances, husbands and wives play a game that Dr. Jampolsky calls "Who is guilty and who is innocent."[8] He says that the game begins when one marriage partner attempts to throw a "hot potato" of guilt to the other one. The guilt is then thrown back and forth, with each partner saying, "You're guilty," "No, you're guilty," and so on.

In marriages where one of the partners is a defeated perfectionist, the game doesn't take very long to play, and goes more like this: "You're guilty." "You're right, I'm guilty!"

What should you do when people are trying to push your guilt buttons? Try to step back and get a fresh perspective on the situation. Try to decide what is motivating you. If it's guilt, make a conscious choice not to give in. You can never tell what someone else's motives may be, but if you sense that someone is trying to manipulate you, and has his finger mighty close to those guilt buttons, proceed with extreme caution.

4. Lower your high-jump bar of life. The sooner you realize you can't be perfect, the sooner you'll stop letting guilt have a stranglehold over you.

If you find yourself thinking about the failures and rejections you have suffered, make a conscious effort to change things. You have experienced triumphs and won victories in your life. Think about those: Last week when your boss told you he enjoyed your presentation; that new dessert you made that the Walkers liked so much; that spelling bee you won in the seventh grade—dwell on the successes and not on the failures.

You may be an average woman who'll never be mistaken for Jennifer Aniston or Halle Berry—or an average Joe who won't ever have his name plastered across the sports page headlines like Tom Brady or Michael Jordan. But don't go around comparing yourself to Julia Roberts or Michael Jordan, measuring your successes by theirs. You can always get yourself into trouble by comparing yourself with other people, or even by comparing the way you are against the way you'd really like to be. Remember that there will be many people who do greater things than you, and many who will not begin to match your accomplishments. But the person who is controlled by guilt has a distorted view, in which he can see only those who are better than he.

I tell many of my women clients that I believe it would be easier to be a saint such as Mother Teresa than to be the "perfect" wife and mother. "Try being the most loving wife you can be and everything else will fall into line," I tell them.[9]

146

So lower that high-jump bar of life. Be content with singles instead of home runs. Find joy in compliments from your husband and children instead of dreaming of earning an international honor or an Academy Award. (Yes, I realize I'm oversimplifying here. I know of very few people who feel discouraged because they've never won the Nobel Prize or an Academy Award, but the principle still applies. You are a good person with many outstanding qualities. Lower your expectations for yourself and center on what you have done instead of what you haven't done.)

I'll go into more detail on how you can lower that high-jump bar of life in the next chapter.

5. Stop living by the other person's agenda. Let's stop for a moment and take a little quiz. You do love quizzes, don't you?

(That question, in itself, may be a good test of whether you live by someone else's agenda. Because a person who did, would probably say, "Oh, sure, I love quizzes," even if he hated them, just because he knew that was what the other person wanted.)

In the following quiz, give yourself 4 points for each *always* answer, 3 points for *usually*, 2 for *seldom*, and 1 for *never*.

A. When your family goes out to eat, do you choose the restaurant?_____.

B. If you really liked a blouse (or shirt), but your best friend didn't, would you buy it anyway?_____.

C. If you wanted to spend your vacation at the mountains and your spouse wanted to go to the seashore, would you wind up going to the mountains?_____.

D. If you wanted to spend your vacation at the mountains and your spouse wanted to go to the seashore, would you even tell your spouse about your wishes?_____.

E. If your neighbor wanted you to baby-sit her two-year-old for a couple of hours, but it was inconvenient for you, would you tell her no?_____.

F. If you were asked to serve on a committee, but you were on three other committees and didn't feel as if you could handle another one, would you explain your feelings and ask to be excused from the new committee?_____.

G. In a restaurant, if you order a steak well-done and it is brought to you rare, would you send it back?_____.

H. In a restaurant, if you order roast beef and the waiter brings you fried shrimp, would you sent it back?_____.

I. A colleague at work invites you to a Tupperware party at her house. It's the third one you've been invited to this month, and you really don't feel like another one. Would you politely turn down her invitation?_____.

J. A co-worker is always slacking off, palming off his work on you. Would you confront him about his behavior?_____.

Okay, let's see how you scored:

40 points—You have a really strong self-image. You live your life by nobody's agenda but your own! People probably have a nice nickname for you. Something like "little Attila."

30–39 points—You don't seem to have any problem either. You temper your own desires with concern about other people's feelings, but you're not afraid to stick up for yourself.

25–29 points—Well, you're on the borderline here. Not overly aggressive, but not a washout either.

20–24 points—It's not easy for you to stick up for yourself. More often than not, you find yourself living life by the other person's rules.

13–19 points—You need to make some changes in your approach to life. Your desires *do* matter, and you need to learn to express them.

11–12 points—Well, at least you were able to send back the shrimp when what you really ordered was roast beef. That's not much, but at least it's a start. Drastic changes are needed in your self-image.

10 points—People have a nickname for you, too: "Doormat."

It takes a lot of effort for the guilty defeated perfectionist to stop living according to the other person's agenda. But for your own good you simply must force yourself to make the change. If your friends and loved ones really care about you, they will begin to enter into a healthy give-and-take relationship with you. It may take a while, especially if they have been used to doing all the taking and letting you do the giving. But stick to your guns, and things will change.

6. Stop kicking yourself around. More specifically, stop beating all those dead horses. Quit spending your time watching instant replays of all the mistakes you've made. Remember that everyone makes mistakes, and you're bound to make several more before you find yourself in heaven.

Stop viewing yourself as worthless, helpless, and hopeless, and see yourself as a worthy human being, created by God. Learn to major on your strengths instead of your weaknesses.

Do your best to ignore criticism and try not to let it get you down. What makes you think those critics know more than you do anyway?

Consider what the *Chicago Times* said about Abraham Lincoln's Gettysburg Address: ". . . silly, flat, and dishwatery utterances. . . ."[10] Those who criticize you could be every bit as far off the mark.

7. Learn to "call an audible" at the line of scrimmage. Those of you who are football fans know what it means to "call an audible." For the rest of you, let me explain. In a football game, the offensive team goes into a huddle and chooses the play it's going to run.

However, when play is ready to start, if the quarterback sees something in the defensive alignment which causes him to think the selected play won't work, he may decide to call an audible. That means he yells out a series of signals that changes the play.

So, what I'm saying is this—when you find yourself in a situation that has always caused you to react poorly, call a time-out, step back, and analyze the situation, and then change the play. What would the "old" you do? But that always got you into trouble. What should the "new" you do?

If you learn to stop and think situations through, you'll be less likely to be motivated by guilt. And the less you operate on the basis of guilt, the better you'll feel about yourself, and the less you'll need to be motivated by guilt!

Remember that you don't have to be perfect. That's not what you're aiming for. You must learn to admit and accept that you are imperfect, and that you always will be.

But remember, too, that imperfections can sometimes be helpful. They may draw people to you, help people relate to you, and so on.

Everybody identifies with a little imperfection!

6

Is It Time to Lower Your High-Jump Bar of Life?

We've been talking quite a bit in this book about rejection, failure, and the inability to measure up. More specifically we've been talking about those people known as defeated perfectionists. These are people who can never bring themselves to settle for merely being excellent. They want to be perfect.

One thing I've mentioned about the defeated perfectionist is that his successes never satisfy him. If he succeeds, he immediately tells himself the goal he set wasn't tough enough. Otherwise, he never would have been able to do it! This is what I call raising the "high-jump bar of life."

You know by now that I really love sports, and as a psychologist, I see many competitions and events in the sports world which are analogous to daily life. Every time I see the high jump in a track meet, I think of the defeated perfectionist.

Here comes the high jumper, running as fast as he can. At the last minute he pushes himself up . . . and over the bar. He's cleared eight feet!

What happens next? The bar is raised a quarter of an inch, and another quarter, and so on, until there is only one competitor left. All of the others have failed in their attempts to get over the bar at that height. Of course, if none of the competitors could get over the bar when it was at six feet, it would be lowered.

Here comes the defeated perfectionist . . . huffing and puffing . . . arms flying as he speeds toward the high-jump bar. Now he's up, and up . . . and over!

Immediately, he's up and yelling at the officials:

"Hey, what's wrong with this thing?"

"What do you mean? There's nothing wrong with it!"

"There must be! I got over it, didn't I! Raise it up another six inches!"

"Six inches? Why—"

"No, wait, Raise it another foot!"

So the bar goes up another foot.

Here he comes again, putting everything he has into the jump. Only this time he fails to make it.

"Leave it where it is. I'm going to try again."

And again, he fails.

"Maybe we should lower it a little bit," suggests one of the officials.

"Nothing doing. I'm going to clear this bar if it kills me!"

And it probably will. Time after time after time he tries without success to clear the bar. He's exhausted, he's bruised, and he's angry. But still, he won't listen to a single word about lowering the bar.

In my mind's eye, I can see him, late at night, after the crowds and all of the other competitors have already gone home. He's running much slower now and not jumping nearly as high. I hear the clank of the high-jump bar as it falls to the ground one more time.

It is, to be sure, a sad, pathetic picture, but it's not as much of an exaggeration as you might think. For this is the way the defeated perfectionist operates.

He reaches for the stars when planets are within reach, he wants to drive a Cadillac when he can only afford a Volkswagen, and—to use another sports analogy—he is never content with singles but wants to hit a home run every time he gets up to the plate.

The really sad thing about it is that he isn't even aware that he's placing all these unreasonable demands on himself. And, he has a distorted view of reality. When he looks about him, he sees a world populated with successful people—men and women who do seem to hit home runs every time they're up to bat. He sees his own successes as minuscule, while his failures are so large and obvious that they dwarf the Grand Canyon by comparison.

He wants to be among the successful ones, and so he keeps raising that high-jump bar, thereby sabotaging his chances to be successful at anything. For instance, suppose the defeated perfectionist is in a staff meeting, where his boss asks him if he will please prepare a report on Widget sales in the southeastern United States for review in a meeting the following week.

Then the boss turns to Krelman. "And, Krelman, I'd like you to do the same regarding the northeastern states."

Mr. DP says, "Wait a minute, boss. I can handle that, too. No need to tie up Krelman on this."

The boss is incredulous. "Are you sure? That's a pretty tall order."

"Oh, sure. No big deal."

Of course, as soon as the meeting is over, he realizes what he's done to himself.

He could have handled the southeastern report just fine. But now he has way too much to do. He's filled with doubts, and he begins to panic. He thinks he won't do the sort of job the boss wants, and because of this he's afraid to do anything. He can't seem to get started. The final result is not only that he doesn't get the northeastern section of the report done, but does a slipshod, poorly documented report on the Southeast.

He's sabotaged himself again. (And a good guess is his family will pay for it in more ways than one.)

Now, chances are that you're sitting there reading this and thinking to yourself: *Well, he's certainly not talking about me.* But I have to ask you, are you sure about that?

You may not do it in such obvious ways, but do you subconsciously keep raising your high-jump bar of life—and stacking the deck against yourself?

You see, well-meaning people have always told you that you should set your goals "way out there" somewhere. If you set a goal that's easily attainable, they say, you'll never stretch yourself to your maximum limit . . . you'll never know the great things you might have accomplished. But if you have goals that are really just beyond your reach, you'll always keep developing, improving, and accomplishing beyond what you ever thought you'd do.

Well . . . although it might smack of heresy, I'm telling you right now to forget that kind of thinking. You ought to set goals for yourself, yes, and they ought to challenge you to do your best. But if they're totally unrealistic, all those goals serve to do is keep you frustrated, defeated, and rejected!

For example, it wouldn't be an exaggeration to say that most little boys have dreams of playing major league sports. They see themselves pitching a no-hit ball game to win a World Series, running fifty yards for a touchdown that wins the Super Bowl, or hitting a desperation basket just as the buzzer sounds to capture the NBA crown. Very few people, no matter how hard they might try, will ever be able to make it into professional sports. Even for those who do, the goal of winning a championship is elusive.

Now, a goal like that is fine when you're a little boy. But if you're a thirty-five-old accountant, still playing sandlot ball and hoping that a scout for the Boston Red Sox is going to notice you—well, you're living in a dreamworld. It's time to face reality and readjust your goals.

No, I don't imagine there are really too many thirty-five-old accountants hoping for a shot at major league baseball, but I think you can understand my point. Your goals, to be effective and beneficial for you, must be within your range of possibilities.

Another thing defeated perfectionists often are guilty of is expecting too much of themselves too soon. They're not willing to pay their dues and take one step at a time. They want to hit it big and hit it big now, and they're not content with success at smaller levels.

Looking for Overnight Success

How often do you read about people who have become "overnight" successes? It happens all the time in the entertainment industry. Some young woman bursts into the spotlight. She's on the cover of *Newsweek*, interviewed by Barbara Walters, and everybody in the world seems to know her name. Six months ago, nobody had ever heard of her.

But look a little closer. She's been in dozens of plays on the community theater level. She's studied acting for years. She's landed a bit part here, been on a couple of TV shows, and then a low-budget movie. In other words, her "overnight" success hasn't come overnight at all. It's been one step at a time, climbing up the ladder rung by rung. She has succeeded at one level before moving on to the next.

Yes, I admit there are exceptions to this rule. If you were around in the fifties you're bound to remember a young singer named Fabian. How did Fabian hit the big time? Legend has it that he was sitting on the porch in front of his house in Philadelphia when a record producer happened to go by. He took one look at the young man and realized he had "star quality." It didn't matter whether he could sing—he couldn't, in fact—because he had that look. Fabian had hit records, he made movies, and he was greeted by throngs of screaming teen girls wherever he went.

But like most overnight sensations, Fabian's star burned brightly for a year or two and then faded from sight. Those whose success lasts are those who enjoy a steady, slow climb to the top.

The attitude of wanting to be an immediate success carries over into other areas of the defeated perfectionist's life.

For instance, if Roger has fifteen things to do around the house, he'll have a tendency to want to get them all done at once.

Perhaps he'll even draw up a list:

Things to Do Today

Fix the leaky faucet in the bathroom.

Clean the garage.

Redo the weatherstripping on the front door.

Prune the trees in the backyard.

Mow the lawn.

Fertilize the rose bushes.

Paint the trim on the front porch awning.

Replace the broken boards on the back fence.

Repair the broken chain on Susie's bike.

Fix the belt on the food processor.

Change the car's oil.

And on and on. He may have fifteen or twenty things on that list. And then he has another list for work, with just as many items on it.

Now it certainly doesn't take a genius to know he'll never be able to get all of those things done in a single day. It's more likely that he won't get anything on his list done. Instead, he'll spin between them. He doesn't even have them prioritized, so he doesn't know which he needs to do first.

Perhaps he'll start out in the garage:

"It sure does need to be cleaned up." But then the remembers that the lawn needs to be mowed. "I'd better do that now, before it gets too hot (or too cold, or too dark)."

So he goes and gets the lawn mower. But as he's wheeling it out of the garage he sees the car and remembers that he really wants to change the oil. When he goes to get the oil, he sees the can of paint sitting there and remembers the front porch.

What in the world should he do first? His head is spinning and he feels overwhelmed. He just has much too much to do!

Before he knows it, the day's over and he hasn't been able to get anything done. Oh, he's started several of the things on his list—he just hasn't been able to get any of them completed.

So, with a sigh, he goes in and prepares another list. He takes out his paper and his pen and writes:

Things to Do Tomorrow

Fix the leaky faucet in the bathroom.

Clean the garage.

And so on.

He may write that same list, day after day after day, always feeling overwhelmed, never getting very much accomplished.

Is he doing anything right? Actually, the answer is yes. Making a list of things to do is a good idea. (That's especially true as I find myself getting older, and sometimes having trouble remembering what I'm supposed to do unless I've written it down somewhere.) If you feel overwhelmed by all of the tasks confronting you, keep a list so you can keep track of them all. But keep that list as short as possible, with the "to-do's" spread over a sufficient amount of time.

What Roger has done wrong is that he tried to cram every single thing onto one list, into one day's time, and he can't possibly get everything done that way. As a matter of fact, he sometimes went for days without crossing a single thing off his list. Instead, he wound up moving the items from day to day, seeing his list grow longer instead of shorter.

The same thing would be true of his "work" list. He wanted to get everything done right now, but you don't have to get everything done on Monday!

Instead, the must-do items should have been spread evenly throughout the week. If Roger's list were exceptionally long, some of the items might even be placed in the next week, or, if they weren't that pressing, the week after that.

Part of the reason the defeated perfectionist wants to get everything done right now is that he's afraid he's going to slip up and forget something. ("I'm such a goof-up, and if I don't write it down I'm probably going to forget.") So write it down, but write it down for next Wednesday instead of this afternoon!

Sometimes you simply have to call "time out," step back, and take the time to sort out your priorities. (I take little fishing trips to New York.) Decide what you can and cannot do. And if you are the type who's always getting himself in a tight spot, you may need to call time out every few days—perhaps even every day—until you learn to lower that high-jump bar a bit!

And when you do call a time out, spend a little while sorting out priorities. Ask yourself some questions.

"Do I really have to do this today . . . or tomorrow, or even this week?"

"Which is more important: finishing this report or setting up that staff meeting?"

"Is there anything on my list that's unrealistic or unnecessary? Am I expecting too much of myself, or taking on responsibility for things I'm not really expected to do?"

It's also a good idea to number the things you have to do in order of their importance. And then stick with that order and do first things first!

Florence was an intelligent, hard-working woman who, nevertheless, couldn't seem to get anything accomplished. At the end of the day, she'd look back over what she'd done—and there was nothing there.

"And I really don't understand it," she complained, "because I'm soooo busy!"

And she was busy! She raced through her day like a hundred-miles-an-hour hurricane. It is hard to imagine so much energy being dispensed with so little effect.

"What am I doing wrong?" She was desperate for an answer—and it didn't take long to find it.

Florence was one of those people who carried a list around with twenty-five or more "things to do" on it. What's more, she never took the time to sift through the list and prioritize.

But there was an even bigger problem. Florence didn't even realize that she was a defeated perfectionist. She had an innate fear of messing things up, and so she avoided the larger, more important tasks to concentrate on the smaller matters. As a result, she often found herself pushed up against next-to-impossible deadlines, sometimes staying at the office until nearly midnight, or else taking her work home. She always figured that she did her best work when her back was up against the wall, but the truth was that it was only when she had to choose between two scary choices—doing the work or losing her job—that she opted to do the work. She often missed deadlines, and only the fact that everybody, including her boss, seemed to like her saved her job.

She denied it at first, but then as she really began to analyze her activities, she could see that almost all of her time was taken up with the trivial. She'd sit down at her desk to start working on an important matter—and then she'd see the three messages from people wanting her to call them back.

She'd fool herself by saying, "Well, if I get these phone calls taken care of, then I can concentrate on the really important things."

But after the phone calls, she'd go through the mail, and find a couple of items that just "begged" for her immediate attention, so she'd spend the next forty-five minutes or so drafting her responses.

Then Jane would come in with a personal problem, and well, of course Florence wouldn't want to be rude when Jane needed a friend to talk to. After that, another couple of phone calls, and perhaps Harold from the office next door would come in and ask her advice on his project. (She was always happy to give it because it really wasn't her responsibility, which meant that she wasn't as afraid of it as she was of the things she *was* responsible for.)

And so it would go throughout the entire day. More phone calls, more "urgent" mail to handle, more visitors, more "emergencies" to take care of—though they were rarely her emergencies. She was a great one when it came to shuffling paper, rearranging her files to make them more "efficient," and typing dozens of memorandums on various subjects.

She finally realized that she had to force herself to change her ways. If a major project needed her attention, everything else would have to wait. Those phone calls could be returned later. And, as far as catching up on her correspondence, she learned to set aside Friday mornings for that. Regarding the interruptions by co-workers, she learned to tape a note on her door: "Sorry, but I'm on a tight deadline. Can't talk right now."

It wasn't easy for Florence to change her habits. It never is easy. But she made the effort and she was ultimately successful.

Not only did her productivity increase, but she found that she had more free time. She rarely stayed at the office past six o'clock and never took work home. The things that couldn't be fitted into her old fifty-five-hour workweek were coming close now to fitting into a forty-hour week.

Another good idea Florence put into practice was leaving one day a week blank in her calendar. This, then, became her catch-up day, giving her some breathing room and allowing her to catch up on any "unfinished business" from the rest of the week.

That is an excellent idea for those who tend to bite off more than they can chew. In this way, you can clean up the leftover items from your week's list and not carry them over into the next week. One of the problems for the defeated perfectionist is that he tends to let things pile up to the point where he is completely overwhelmed.

It may be that you want to prepare more than one list. Perhaps you could have a list of Things to Do This Week, another one for Things to Do This Month, and then, for your long-range goals, Things to Do This Lifetime or, at least My Goals for the Next Five Years. Or maybe you would want to keep a list of things to do at work and another of things to do at home. This would be a way to keep both lists short. Otherwise, the defeated perfectionist might pull out his list at work, see ten things that need to be done at home, and spend the rest of his day fretting about them, or vice versa. But whatever you do, don't overwhelm yourself, and don't trade slavery to inertia for slavery to a list.

And don't make the mistake of adding every little thing you have to do to your list. This is another mistake some people make. Once they start keeping a list, they don't know what to put on it and what to leave off. There's no need to keep a list like this:

List of Things to Do Today

Get out of bed
Go potty
Brush my teeth
Take a shower

Eat breakfast

Shave

And so on.

Of course, I'm being facetious, although some people make lists that are almost this detailed. Basically, your list should be to remind you of the items you might otherwise overlook or forget.

So make a list, but make sure the list is working for you instead of the other way around. Don't let the list run your life, and don't let it become a burden. Use it to help you keep things under control, and don't be afraid to chuck the whole thing out the window every once in a while if it suits your purposes. In other words, don't be afraid to allow for flexibility in your schedule.

In *The Birth Order Book* I told about my counseling sessions with another man who got so bogged down in details he couldn't get anything done.[1] The situation came to a head when he got himself into trouble with the Internal Revenue Service. It seems that he hadn't filed his income tax returns in four years.

Was he a criminal, someone out to deliberately cheat the government? Not at all. Actually, he simply hadn't gotten around to it—and this despite the fact that he kept the most minute, detailed financial records of anyone I've ever met!

One room of his house had two picnic tables in it, and both of those tables were completely covered with receipts, notes, and bills of sale.

The problem was—and this again is a delaying tactic often used by the defeated perfectionist—that he had overwhelmed himself with information and had no idea where to start with the process of sifting through it. So for four years, he hadn't done a thing!

His wife was beside herself, not only because of the pending problem with the IRS, but because her husband handled almost everything with the same attention he gave his taxes.

"George, when are you going to fix the toaster?"

"I'll do it tomorrow."

"We have a leaky faucet in the hall bathroom."

"Oh, yeah. I'll take a look at it tomorrow."

That was always his answer. He was always going to get around to it "tomorrow," only tomorrow never came! He was in the position of treading water, making a lot of noise and thrashing around, but not really going anywhere. All the while, the number of things needing his immediate attention had grown from a small hill into a Mount Everest of neglect!

I was finally able to get George to change his ways, to lower his high-jump bar of life by taking things one step at a time. He came to realize that he didn't need to drown himself in details and that he had to commit himself to getting one thing done at a time. If the toaster needed to be fixed, he could work on that Monday evening. Tuesday, he'd work on the leaky faucet, and so on, until he got everything done.

As far as the IRS was concerned, there was nothing to be done but roll up those sleeves and dive in. When he finally got up enough courage to do just that, guess what he discovered?

The IRS had owed *him* money all along!

What would you do if you were married to a fellow like George? How would you move him off square one and get him to *do* something? There are two possible approaches, and both really came into play in George's life.

The first approach would be to let him go ahead and mess things up really good—and then face the consequences. With George, that approach didn't produce any results for at least four years, because the problem was getting worse and worse, and you can't have much more motivation than having the IRS on your back. But this situation did ultimately make George realize that he had to change his ways and sent him to me looking for help.

The second approach would be to walk him through the tasks at hand. Show him how he could tackle one project at a time, that the tasks confronting him aren't really so overwhelming. Once he has the knack of moving along a step at a time instead of a mile at a time, he should be okay.

When it comes to making a record of the tasks confronting you, one question you should always ask yourself is *Is my list reasonable?* If it's not—if you can't possibly get through all the items on it in the allotted time—then rewrite it. If you don't have any room to move things around, then ask yourself what's wrong.

Are you taking on too much responsibility?

Is your boss asking you to do more than you can possibly handle?

What steps can I take to give myself more flexibility and freedom?

Then, don't be afraid to ask for advice and help from others. For instance, you can ask for an appointment with your supervisor. Then sit down with him and go over your job description. Perhaps you have a misunderstanding of the tasks you are supposed to handle. Or perhaps he doesn't realize how much he is asking of you and can delegate some of that responsibility to your co-workers.

Or perhaps the reverse is true. It could be that you are not delegating authority to others, but rather trying to take everything upon your own shoulders and do it yourself. This may be because you have a need to prove yourself, by doing everything on your own, or perhaps it's because you have never learned how to delegate to others. (You may be afraid they'll resent you for dumping work on them, or that your children may resent having to do more of the work around the house, etc.)

The defeated perfectionist is often trying to be a superhero, when things would go much better for him and everyone else concerned if he could simply learn a thing or two about team-work—sharing the work to be done.

As a longtime resident of Tucson, Arizona, I have been a supporter of the athletic programs at the University of Arizona. I have especially enjoyed watching the success of the Wildcats basketball team under the direction of Lute Olsen.

In 1988, the U of A team was one of the best in the school's history, and certainly one of the top collegiate teams in the country. There were some mighty fine players on that team—young men such as Anthony Cook, Sean Elliott, and Steve Kerr. But none of those players was an absolute superstar, someone who carries the entire team all by himself.

The Wildcats rolled over opponent after opponent on their way to the NCAA championship tournament. But they did it on the basis of teamwork. They played together as an unselfish unit, with each man doing his part—looking for the open man, getting the ball inside to the one with the easiest shot, and so on. There were no gunners or ball-hogs. Everyone seemed more interested in the good of the team than his own statistics. And there really was a superstar—Sean Elliott—but to his credit he was a team player all the way.

An important lesson about life could be learned from watching that team in action!

More specifically, what a lesson for the defeated perfectionist who feels as if he has the weight of the world upon his shoulders! He hasn't learned that he's part of a team, and that nobody in the world, with the single exception of himself, expects him to handle everything all alone!

Let me make it clear, at this point, that there is a major difference between the guy who's always trying to hit a home run, always swinging for the fences, and the one who merely tries to take on more than he can handle. Both are defeated perfectionists, yes, and both need to lower their high-jump bar of life. But their motives are vastly different.

I was asked to appear on a broadcast of the "Oprah Winfrey Show" that dealt with the "black sheep" of families. Specifically, the show was asking why some children, in otherwise perfectly normal families, turn out to be troublemakers, rebels, and more generally, the cause of heartbreak and disappointment for their mothers and fathers.

One young man on the show kept insisting that he had "borrowed" five thousand dollars from his father, even though the father didn't know his son had "borrowed" the money, and the rest of the family clearly viewed the matter as a theft.

Why did he "borrow" the money? To invest it in another of a long line of risky business deals. He fully intended to pay it back when he made his fortune, only that didn't happen—and he wound up losing the money.

He was so wrapped up in his own version of reality, and so convincing in his argument that he had merely borrowed the money, that I was almost beginning to believe him.

But I knew that I was looking at a young man who wasn't content to move along in a steady progression. He believed in the words of the late Jim Morrison of The Doors, who sang, "We want the world, and we want it now!"[2]

He was always looking for that big business deal where he was going to make a killing and be set for life. But instead of finding fame and fortune, he just got himself further and further into debt. When the other members of his family finally came to the realization that their help was only enabling him to get deeper into trouble, they stopped bailing him out of tight situations. So he began to help himself by "borrowing" from his father.

Here was a young man who was more than willing to trade what could have been a really decent reality to live in a dream world. He had a lot going for him. He was intelligent, good-looking, and had a supportive family. He undoubtedly could have made something of his life. But he had never learned that success seldom comes overnight and, unless he radically changes his ways, he is condemned to a life of continuing frustration and failure. He'll be a disappointment to everyone he comes in contact with, including himself.

Somehow, though, he has come to believe that he doesn't count for anything unless he's knocking the ball over the fence, and so he'll go through life swinging for the fences. He's forgetting, of course, that baseball players who always try to hit home runs wind up striking out a lot more often than they do hitting the ball out of the park.

He needs to lower that high-jump bar of life—to understand that Superman was the only one who could ever leap over tall buildings in a single bound, and he exists only in the world of fantasy.

What about you? Are you making unreasonable demands on yourself? Are you trying to clear a seven-foot bar before you've even managed a four-foot jump? If so, you need to lower the high-jump bar of your life, and there are several concrete things you can do to help yourself.

I want to talk more specifically about six of them:

1. Learn that there is a difference between excellence and perfection.
2. See your failures as learning experiences upon which to build a better future.
3. Live in the real world.
4. Take a realistic look at yourself.
5. Face up to your fears.
6. Take responsibility for your actions.

Let's go over these items one at a time:

1. Learn that there is a difference between excellence and perfection. The defeated perfectionist is never satisfied with mere excellence. He wants everything to be perfect and can find flaws with just about everything he does.

He may have the gifts of a Leonardo da Vinci, but will still say, as da Vinci did, "I have offended God and mankind because my work didn't reach the quality it should have."[3]

The problem, for Leonardo da Vinci, certainly wasn't within his work, but within his attitude about that work.

I often tell my clients that life is not a gymnastic meet. There are not five judges out there waiting to hold up their scorecards after everything you do.

And, unless you are a major league baseball player your mistakes are not likely to make the pages of the local newspaper. Fortunately, there are no box scores of the daily lives of ordinary people, showing how we booted the ball or threw wildly, allowing the opponent's winning run to score. Then, too, unless you're a presidential candidate your mistatements and misjudgments aren't likely to wind up as the hot topic on ABC's "Nightline" program.

You simply don't have to go through life running up a perfect score in everything you do!

There are eight major differences between the perfectionist and the person who is legitimately pursuing excellence.

— The perfectionist reaches for impossible goals, whereas the pursuer of excellence enjoys meeting high standards that are within his reach.

— The perfectionist bases his values of himself upon his accomplishments, while the person who pursues excellence values himself simply for who he is.

— The perfectionist may be defeated by disappointment. He may give up and surrender, whereas the pursuer of excellence, although disappointed and hurt, will keep moving toward his goal.

— The perfectionist is often devastated by failure, but the pursuer of excellence will learn from it.

— The perfectionist tends to remember his past mistakes and dwell on them. He is convinced that everyone else remembers them, too. The pursuer of excellence, on the other hand, will correct his mistakes, learn the lessons they have to offer, and then forget about them.

— The perfectionist is only happy with being number one. He would feel like a failure if he were in second place out of 100. The pursuer of excellence is happy with himself when he knows he has tried his hardest.

— The perfectionist hates criticism, while the pursuer of excellence welcomes it and seeks to benefit from it.

— The perfectionist has to win to have a high self-esteem, while the pursuer of excellence can finish second and still maintain a healthy self-image.[4]

Which are you—defeated perfectionist or pursuer of excellence? If you see yourself more in the description of the perfectionist, it is time for you to make a conscious effort to change the way you look at yourself, as well as the way you look at life in general.

I had a friend who could not, would not, dance, even though his wife loved to dance. She would plead with him to take her dancing, but he always came up with an excuse. Either his back hurt, or he was too tired, or he had something more important to do. His wife never pushed or badgered him about his refusal to dance with her, but he knew that she was disappointed.

Finally he admitted to her, and to himself, that the reason he didn't want to take her dancing was that he had never exactly been a carbon copy of Fred Astaire. He felt as if he had the proverbial two left feet, complicated by a profound lack of rhythm.

He just knew that everyone else on the dance floor would be watching him. He could envision the men nudging their ladies and saying, "Hey, get a load of *that* guy!" It would be *Saturday Night Fever* in reverse, and he'd probably wind up being laughed out of the place.

Finally, though, time came for the couple to travel several hundred miles to the twentieth reunion of her high school graduating class. He had reluctantly agreed that, "Yes, I will dance with you at the reunion." After all, he really wouldn't know anybody there, so he couldn't do a lot of harm to his reputation.

When the time came, and those oldie-but-goodie melodies were floating out over the floor, he felt his mouth go dry and his stomach begin to churn. But when his wife smiled across the table at him and reached for his hand, he knew he was trapped. A promise was a promise, and so he had no choice but to hesitantly follow her onto the dance floor.

The first few seconds were sheer terror. He felt his cheeks turn red when he stepped on her foot, and he looked around to see how many people were watching him. What a surprise to find that he wasn't the center of everyone's attention.

He stepped on her foot again.

She smiled and told him he was doing great.

By the time the next song started, he was beginning to relax. He could feel the stiffness leaving his body, and that meant he could move more like a human being than a wooden soldier.

Well, before the evening was over, he was having what could only be described as an incredible time on the dance floor. He still wasn't Fred Astaire, but he realized that he didn't have to be. His wife had never expected that from him.

Besides, he may not have been Fred Astaire, but he wasn't exactly Bozo the Clown out there either. The whole thing had a tremendous effect on his self-confidence, and it carried over into other areas of his life. He was less afraid to attack new challenges and, whereas he had always been reluctant to express his feelings, he became more able to say what was on his mind.

All from a few simple turns around the dance floor.

My point is that you don't have to be perfect, or even among the best, to be successful. If you are letting fear keep you off the dance floor of life, you're missing out on much more than you could possibly know!

Now as far as my friend is concerned, he is becoming a better dancer, although he knows he's never going to win any dance contests. The important thing is that he's not letting the fact that he'll never be the best prevent him from trying, and becoming as good as he can be!

But if you won't settle for anything less than perfection, you're shooting for an impossibility, a fantasy.

Everybody falls short of perfection (Rom. 3:23). So don't worry if you goof things up once in a while. You've got a lot of company—the entire human race!

2. See your failures as learning experiences upon which to build a better future. Which of these statements do you believe?

It doesn't matter whether you won or lost, but how you played the game.[5]

Winning isn't the most important thing—winning is the only thing.[6]

Are you offended that I even asked? You're probably thinking, *Of course, I know that winning isn't as important as being fair and trying your hardest.*

But do you really know that—deep down inside where it counts. And if you do, do you live your life as though you know it? Do you let yourself off the hook if you don't come in first, or do you despise yourself for your failures and promise not to let it happen again?

Let's say that you're a pretty good bowler, and you go down to the neighborhood alley on a Saturday night (after the leagues are through, of course) to roll a few with a friend of yours. You know you're better than he is, and you expect to win by at least twenty pins per game. Only tonight, something's wrong. You're a little bit off, and he's a lot on, and you can't seem to beat him.

When he wins the first game by five pins, you figure that, well, these things happen and you'll get him next time. But he starts off the second game with four strikes in a row and winds up with his first-ever 200 game, thirty pins ahead of you. As for the final game of the series, you might as well forget that. By now you're pressing, trying too hard, and can't seem to do anything right.

Now this is a guy you've probably beaten twenty times in a row, so it's about time for him to turn the tables on you. But how do you feel? Really? Are you smiling while you're dying inside and wishing he'd drop that bowling ball on his foot? Be honest with yourself, now.

Husband, how do you handle it when your wife beats you? Whether it's Chinese checkers, Monopoly, or tennis—is it hard to take? (And I'm expecting the wives to ask themselves the same question.)

If we were all to be completely open and honest with one another, we'd have to admit that none of us likes to lose, and it's harder to lose to some people than to others.

But if you can't shake off the disappointment in a matter of minutes, or if losing makes you so angry that you want to put your fist through the wall, you need to discover that losses and failures in life can be good for you. You can learn from them and build upon them.

If you take every loss personally, it's time for you to lower that high-jump bar of life and face up to the fact that everyone loses from time to time.

It's too bad our society stresses winning the way it does—but you don't have to get caught up in the hysteria. The fact that America places too much emphasis on coming in ahead of the other guy can be seen just by taking a quick look at the college-level sports scene. You'll hear plenty of college presidents saying that academics come first, and sports second. But I've never heard of a major college coach being fired because his players weren't getting an education. But I don't care how clean a program he runs—let him lose a few games too many and he's out the door. Look at the salary of a long-term math or English professor and compare it with that of a winning football coach. Not much of a comparison, I'm afraid. And what prompts a school's alumni to want to give to the old alma mater? A top-notch science program, or a bowl-bound football team? You know the answer to that as well as I do.

I'm not sure whether the college sports scene merely mirrors society's attitudes about winning and losing, or if the winning mania of college and professional sports has carried over into society at large. But either way, it's an unfortunate situation. Because it really *doesn't* matter whether you win or lose. The important thing is how you played the game! (With fairness, integrity, and maximum effort.)

Do you remember Gerry Cooney? He was once one of the top names in the world of boxing, dominating opponent after opponent as he punched his way into a championship fight with Larry Holmes in 1982.

On the night Cooney entered the ring to fight Holmes, he had never been beaten. But with the eyes and ears of much of the world focused upon him, all that was about to change!

He lost, and lost big, to the formidable champion Holmes. At that dark moment, Cooney couldn't think about all of those times when the referee had lifted his hand in victory. All he knew was that he had failed.

"I had never done that before in my life, but at this big mega-thing, this worldwide event, I failed. I felt like I had let everyone down."[7] Cooney was so upset by his moment of failure that he sank into a deep depression. He could not get back into the ring for two years.

He considered himself to be washed-up, a hopeless failure.

Never mind the fact that you have to be one fantastic fighter to get a shot at a world championship. Very few boxers, no matter how good they might be, ever get that far. But Cooney couldn't handle failure, and it nearly destroyed him.

More than twenty years earlier, a boxer named Floyd Patterson lost in another championship bout, this one to a hard-punching Swede named Ingemar Johansson. Patterson's loss was unexpected, and it could have ended his career.

But instead, Patterson analyzed what he had done wrong and took steps to correct the flaws in his approach which had allowed Johansson to defeat him. After months of hard work, he was ready for a rematch. This time, things turned out differently. Patterson won and regained the world crown he had lost to Johansson earlier.

Patterson didn't let his failure overwhelm him. Instead, he learned from it and used it to improve his skills as a boxer.

If you can't deal with defeat or don't ever expect it to come your way, your high-jump bar is way, way too high!

Now, it's always good to look back over the times you have failed and see what you can learn from them. Perhaps failure came your way because you took on more responsibilities than you could reasonably expect yourself to handle. Perhaps you didn't try hard enough or were held back by your own fears. It could be that you did not prepare properly to face the task at hand. If any of these reasons led up to your failure, it will be a rather simple matter for you to change things next time.

But if you are able to take an honest, objective look at the times when you have failed, you may be shocked to see that the fault was not with you. Maybe your boss was guilty of not giving you enough time to do a task properly. Perhaps he gave you wrong or insufficient information and is now expecting you to take the blame for his own mistakes. Could it be that you were forced into a situation where you were asked to perform tasks you are not suited for?

For instance, consider Walter, who wanted desperately to learn how to play the guitar. Unfortunately, he didn't seem to have any musical ability whatsoever. He envied Larry, a man who attended the same church and played the guitar brilliantly.

Whenever a group from the church got together, Larry was sure to bring his guitar along and sing a few songs. He'd get everybody to join in and they'd all be having a great time. Walter thought that Larry was the star of the group and wanted to be more like him. So he signed up to take guitar lessons.

Unfortunately for Walter, he couldn't get the hang of it, so he quit in frustration after the third lesson.

Then one night, not too long after that, as a group of friends was leaving a get-together, Larry's car wouldn't start. He didn't have the slightest idea what was wrong, but Walter did. Walter loved to tinker with cars and had the tools and the know-how to fix just about anything.

He raised the hood on Larry's car, rolled up his shirt sleeves, and went to work. In a matter of minutes, he'd found the problem, corrected it, and had Larry ready to roll.

As Larry got into his car he said, "I really appreciate your help, Walter." And, almost as an afterthought, he added, "I'm a total klutz when it comes to anything mechanical. Glad you were here."

You see, Walter and Larry had different strengths and weaknesses.

Walter, who was a master mechanic, was setting his high-jump bar of life too high when he wanted to be a musician, too. He simply didn't have the aptitude for it.

And Larry, on the other hand, would have been setting his high-jump bar too high if he had wanted to be a mechanic.

Every human being has areas of strength and areas of weaknesses. You are doing yourself an injustice if you concentrate on your weakest areas and overlook your strengths.

There are many lessons to be learned from your failures beyond the obvious one of coming to understand what went wrong so you can avoid doing the same thing next time.

In their book *When Smart People Fail*, Carole Hyatt and Linda Gottlieb talk about some of the lessons to be learned from failure.

They say that failure often gives compassion and humility. It helps us to reorder our priorities, and it sometimes makes us aware that to fail isn't really that bad, thereby emboldening us to take the sort of risks that can lead to success. Finally, they say, failing can give you a sense of power.

What do they mean by this?

You have the power to figure out what went wrong and to correct it.

You have the power to reinterpret what happened to you and put it in the most enabling scenario possible.

You have options before you if you choose to see them. And therefore you have the power to change.[8]

They speak of other powers also. The power to "reinvent" yourself, the power to "declare yourself the judge of what you do," and the "power" to forgive yourself.

These women, both of whom have experienced tremendous successes as well as crushing failures, also have a few words to say about what failure is:

Failure is a judgment about an event.
It is a word used to define a stage.
It is not a condemnation of character.
It is not a permanent condition.
It is not a fatal flaw.
It is not a contagious social disease.
It is a judgment about an event.[9]

3. Live in the real world. Everyone remembers James Thurber's story "The Secret Life of Walter Mitty." Here was a man who couldn't seem to keep his feet firmly on the ground. In the middle of his humdrum daily life, his imagination carried him away to great adventures in which he was usually the hero.

It's a funny story, but what makes it even funnier is the fact that most of us can see ourselves in it. We all daydream and fancy ourselves being heroic in one fashion or another—whether it's hitting a home run in the World Series, being named Miss America, or winning the local talent contest.

Of course, we all know the difference between reality and fantasy and there is nothing wrong with daydreaming. In fact, it can be quite healthy.

But the problem for too many people is that they don't quite know where the dream leaves off and the reality begins. And a major problem for many defeated perfectionists is that they tend to live their lives as Walter Mittys in reverse!

In other words, whereas Walter Mitty always saw himself as the champion and the hero, the defeated perfectionist carries around an unreal vision of himself as the failure and the goof-up.

He tends to see other people as champions and heroes and wonders why he can't be more like them.

But as long as he refuses to face up to life in the real world, he'll remain on the outside, and he'll have to be content with his dreams.

Now life in a dreamworld isn't always pleasant. There are those pleasant dreams, "sweet dreams," that we tell our children to have each night when we kiss them good night. But there are also nightmares—and many a defeated perfectionist lives in a nightmare world of his own making. He dreams that he's a failure, that he's not good enough, that nobody will ever give him a chance, and so forth.

Whatever the case may be, living a fantasy kind of life is never healthful, and even the most wonderful of dreams won't get you anywhere unless you can find a way to make them come true.

There are several ways people can choose to live in fantasy-land, and I want to discuss just a few of these.

A. People live in fantasyland by constantly comparing themselves to others. Remember back in chapter 3 how I talked about the mistake many parents make of comparing their children to one another?

"Why can't you be more like Glenda?"

"Look, dear, at what Marvin did. Remember when Harold did that?"

This sort of thing goes on all the time, unfortunately, but it's not helpful nor healthy. It wasn't good for you when your parents compared you to your other brothers or sisters, it's not good for your children when you make comparisons among them, and it's not good for you when you compare yourself to others.

I'm not talking about momentary flights of fantasy.

It's okay for a woman to lose herself in a daydream wondering what her life would be like if she were Catherine Zeta-Jones or Carmen Electra. Or a man may fantasize from time to time about looking like Brad Pitt or throwing touchdown passes like Tom Brady. That's natural, and it's not harmful . . . unless it becomes an obsession.

When I was a kid, in the mid 1950s, many of the boys I knew wanted to be like one person—Elvis Presley. They wanted sideburns like he had, they wanted to have the same cool sneer that he had, they wanted to play the guitar and sing like he did—but most of all they wanted to have his popularity and his money!

Just think of the impact Elvis Presley had on the world of entertainment! He was the undisputed king of rock 'n' roll and a millionaire many times over. He had everything a man could possibly want—dozens of gold records, a long career in movies, his own personal jet to whisk him across the country whenever the mood struck him, a mansion in Nashville, a beautiful home in Los Angeles, and millions of adoring fans who idolized him.

No wonder all the boys wanted to be like Elvis Presley. But what did all of that get him?

I'll never forget that August day back in 1977. I was driving to my office in Tucson when the news bulletin came over the radio.

"Elvis Presley, the king of rock 'n' roll, is dead at forty-two."

The news shook me so badly I had to pull over to the side of the road. "No way," I said. "He can't be dead!"

But he was.

Later on I began to read about the way Elvis Presley died. I discovered that he had ballooned to a whopping 258 pounds. He had been on drugs. He'd spent his last days on earth as a virtual recluse. Yes, Elvis Presley had it all—fame, fortune, and everything money could buy—but it didn't make him a happy man, nor did it guarantee him a long life on earth.

Do you dream of being like Elvis Presley? Look at what it did for him. And his situation was by no means unique. Those who are able to "have it all" very often find that "all" isn't enough.

If fame and fortune were the twin pillars of success in life, Marilyn Monroe should have been a happy woman. Instead, she took her own life. Judy Garland should have been tremendously happy. She, too, committed suicide.

I could go on with a roster of those who either took their own lives or who died as victims of their own excesses, but it would make for depressing reading, so I won't.

But my point is that you should never wish yourself to be like someone else, or to have what someone else has, because you can't look into that person's soul to see the sorrows and pains he carries around with him from day to day.

Now if it sounds like I'm preaching here—well, I'm sorry about that—but it's preaching worth listening to, so hear me out.

You have within you everything you need to be happy. God didn't want you to be Elvis Presley—or you *would* have been Elvis Presley. And that also means you'd be dead. I'm not trying to be flippant or cruel. But you have already outlived the king of rock 'n' roll. Every breath you take, every pleasure you enjoy is something that Elvis never had.

When my time on earth is over—and my friends and family members gather to pay their last respects—I will consider my life to have been a huge success if my wife can say, "He was a good husband and a good father." What more could anyone ask out of life?

So dream about being Beyonce or Tom Cruise. It's okay to wonder what it would be like. But don't compare your life with the one you think they live. Lower your high-jump bar of life, and remember: You're better off being you. Don't trade the real world for a dream. You might wind up with a nightmare!

B. People live in fantasyland by refusing to make choices that would benefit them in the long run. Do you always seem to make the wrong choices? Are you unlucky in love, career choices, and so on? Does it sometimes seem to you that every turn you take is a wrong turn?

It could be that you are making the wrong choices because you insist on acting upon the advice of your heart instead of your head. In other words, you choose to ignore the signals that what you're doing is wrong because you want to do it so badly.

In the Steve Martin movie *The Man With Two Brains* there is a scene where he has fallen in love with an obviously wicked-hearted woman. He stands in front of a portrait of his first wife, who has passed on to her reward, and says that he would like to be sure he is doing the right thing. If not, he would love to have some kind of sign.

Immediately, the lights in his house begin blinking on and off, the picture begins spinning on the wall, there are eerie sounds of moaning, and a strong wind blows his neatly combed hair into a dozen different directions. All of this continues for at least thirty seconds.

But once it's finished, Martin says that well, since there was no sign, he'll just assume he's doing the right thing. It's a funny scene—and talk about art imitating life!

How many people do you know who pray, "Lord, if there's anything wrong with what I'm doing, please let me know"? And then they quickly slap their hands over their ears so they won't hear His voice telling them it's wrong. Or maybe they pray something like, "God, please close this door if You don't want me to walk through it—but I sure hope You won't close it, because as You know, God, I sure want to walk through it. I'll be disappointed and angry if You don't let me do what I want to do—but go ahead and stop me anyway, because I suppose You might know what's best for me."

Well, they may not really pray a prayer like that one, but God knows that's what they're thinking.

I've said it before, and I tell you again, that if you want to succeed, it is often necessary to go against your feelings—to do things you really don't want to do, and to keep yourself from doing things you do want to do.

In my years as a practicing psychologist, I have counseled many women who are desperately unhappy because they've thrown their lives away on men who are simply no good.

Marjorie will cry because Bill is an alcoholic. He drinks all the time, he can't seem to hold a job, he's abusive to her and the kids, and she doesn't understand what happened to him.

"Didn't you have any idea, before you married him, that he was an alcoholic?"

"Well—I knew he liked to drink. But a lot of men like to drink—and I figured it was something he'd outgrow."

And then there's Ruby, whose husband is violent. He's given her more than one black eye, knocked out a few teeth, and she's had headaches just about every day since the time he hauled off and slugged her on the jaw.

He's always sorry after it happens, and promises that he loves her and won't ever hit her again. And he doesn't—until the next time she does something to make him angry. And she never knows what's going to set him off.

"Before you were married," I ask her, "did you ever have any indication that he could turn violent?"

"Well," she admits, "he did hit me a few times while we were dating. But he was always so apologetic, and so good to me afterward—and I figured that if I married him, I could change him."

Here are two women—attractive, intelligent women—who chose to ignore the signals they were receiving. Both of them should have been able to see what marrying these men would bring them. But they were in love, they wanted to believe things would be different, and so they chose to hide from reality.

What would you do if you were driving along on the freeway at fifty-five miles per hour, and a terrible, clanking noise started coming from under your hood? Would you turn up the volume on the radio so you couldn't hear it anymore and hope it would go away? Of course not. And that's the way it is in every area of life. You can ignore the danger signals that come to you in a variety of ways, but you do so at your own risk. And, one way or another, you're going to be paying some pretty high repair bills later on.

In his book *How to Raise Your Self-Esteem*, Nathaniel Branden talks about choosing to "live consciously" as opposed to "living unconsciously."[10]

He gives several examples of what he means by this, including a discussion of two men, Jim and John, both of whom were hired by the same company.

John immediately set about learning everything he could about his job. He wanted to know how it fit into the overall context of his company, how he could do it more efficiently, and he tried to learn as well as he could what the jobs of his colleagues entailed.

Jim on the other hand, didn't seem to care about anything but doing what was expected of him. He seemed to live for the five o'clock quitting bell and didn't have the slightest idea how what he was doing fit into the big picture, nor did he care.

John, you see, was living consciously, while Jim was living unconsciously. When a higher position opened up, John was promoted, while Jim was passed over. And then an angry Jim wondered why he never had any good luck like old John.

Dr. Branden gives another example of two men, Jerry, who chose to live consciously, and Phillip, who chose to live unconsciously.

In the middle of a heated argument with his wife, Jerry stopped and said, "Wait a minute. I think I'm being defensive and not really hearing you. Could we back up a few steps and try again?"[11]

Phillip, on the other hand, chose to ignore his wife's unhappiness. If she tried to talk to him in the morning he would tell her he couldn't talk because he was on his way to work. Any other time was inappropriate, too. Then one day, when he came home from work, he found a note telling him that she just couldn't take it anymore and that she had left him. And he couldn't believe it. How could she leave like this, without giving him a chance?

If you are living unconsciously, you are living in fantasyland and not paying attention to the signals reality is sending you.

I'm not saying every bad thing that happens to you is a result of your inattention. Not at all. Sometimes, through no fault of your own, you'll find yourself in a no-win situation. No one can tell with certainty when the stock market will rise or fall. The company you work for may make some bad choices, land in financial trouble, and be forced to cut back. People do change, and someone you love may suddenly become abusive. These things happen in life. But if you pay attention to the signals and keep your eyes open, they will happen to you much less often.

In his book, Dr. Branden lists several ways you can live consciously. These include:

Thinking, even when thinking about something may be difficult.

Making every effort to see things clearly, whether or not this comes easily or naturally.

Having a respect for reality, whether or not it's painful, as opposed to a desire to avoid reality.

Being willing to take appropriate risks, even when you are afraid..

Dealing honestly with yourself.

Living in and being responsible to the present, rather than retreating into a fantasy world.

Having a willingness to see and correct your past mistakes, rather than continuing in error.[12]

To these, I would add something I've mentioned before—the willingness to go against your feelings—to act with your head instead of your heart.

I need to say a few words here to the type of person who is more than likely to get into all sorts of trouble for following his heart instead of his head—and that's the "hopeless romantic." When it comes to a love relationship between a man and a woman, some people are quite simply afraid to open their eyes and use their brains because it seems to "cheapen" everything.

They may like the feeling of being in love (and I agree, it is a pretty special feeling). They know their lives are out of control, but they tell themselves they can't help it.

I'm always hearing things like, "I was just swept into it," or, "I knew he wasn't good for me, but I couldn't help myself."

I can't begin to count the times I've talked to women (and men, too) who became involved in extramarital affairs because they "just couldn't help it."

"I never intended to cheat on Eric, but Floyd and I were just drawn to each other. It was irresistible. It was overpowering—and neither one of us could do anything about it."

I would hate to be accused of being unromantic, but I have to say this about that: bullcrumble!

To fall in love is to make a conscious decision to do so. You may tell yourself, *Oh, I'm not going to have anything to do with this. I won't think about it, and I won't plan anything, and then I'll just see what happens.*

But you're lying to yourself, because you are thinking about it, wondering what's going to happen, and probably hoping that something will. You're making a conscious decision to think about that person, to be with that person, and thereby to tempt yourself to get deeper and deeper into the relationship.

Let me say again that I believe romantic love is wonderful. I love my wife, Sande, very much and honestly don't know how I would get along in life without her. But a love affair between a man and woman has to involve the intellect as well as the emotions. If yours doesn't, you could be headed for more trouble than a snowblower salesman in the middle of the Arizona desert.

You could wind up married to someone who is not good in any way for you or become involved in an illicit affair that winds up costing you dearly, or become so emotionally involved in a relationship that you are totally devastated when reality does finally break through and the romance ends.

Any of these situations would cause you a great deal of pain, as well as the loss of your self-respect.

So be careful. Don't be afraid to give your heart away, but don't do it without a great deal of forethought!

C. People live in fantasyland by living in the past. This is a particular problem for the defeated perfectionist, who often measures his life in terms of the times he has failed.

"Why, I know I'll never be able to learn how to drive. My dad tried to teach me back in '57, and I just couldn't get the hang of it. I felt so stupid, and I made myself a promise that I wouldn't ever try again. No, sir, I'll just walk the rest of my life."

Or, "I'll never ask another girl for a date as long as I live. Why, I asked Mary Lou Jones when we were both freshmen in high school, and she told me she couldn't go because she had to stay home and wash her hair. I could see by the look in her eyes that she was lying to me. She just didn't want to go out with me, and she was almost insulted that I asked her. Right then and there I said to myself, *I'm just going to be single for the rest of my life.* That's all there is to it."

Ridiculous examples? Perhaps. But not much more ridiculous than many of the excuses I've heard from otherwise intelligent people.

Whatever bad has happened to you in the past needs to stay there—in the past. It has no bearing on your life today and you must make every effort not to let it hold you back.

When you make a mistake, take the time to go back over what you did wrong. Try to learn from it, to see where you made the wrong choice. But once you've done that and derived every benefit you can from it, then leave it alone. And don't base your actions today on the things that happened to you yesterday.

You know what they say about someone who falls off a horse. The best thing he can do is get right back in the saddle. That's good advice—and not only for those who are taking riding lessons! The old saw says that it is not a disgrace to fall, but it is a disgrace to lie there.

Everyone falls, everyone fails, and there has never been a human being who has not been plagued with self-doubts at one time or another. But those who overcame were the ones who kept on reaching toward the future and who were willing to leave their pasts behind them.

In chapter 8, I'll spend a little time telling you about several of these "great failures" of history, but right now let me just quote from a letter a publishing house sent to a struggling would-be author:

> You've wasted enough of our time with your junk. You can't write, you never could write, and you will never be able to write.[13]

Harsh words indeed. What would you do if you received a letter like that. Most people would probably let it stop them in their tracks. "I guess I'm not cut out to be a writer. Might as well go into the real estate business or something."

But the man who received this letter wasn't going to let past failures keep him from reaching for future success. He wasn't about to live in the past.

His name? Zane Grey, one of the most prolific novelists of the twentieth century—a man who published dozens of Western novels and sold millions upon millions of them!

D. People live in fantasyland by refusing to accept anything but no for an answer. One of my favorite old television shows is "The Bob Newhart Show," on which Newhart portrays a psychologist.

One of the characters on the show was a mousey, soft-spoken little man who had the inferiority complex to end all inferiority complexes. He was a door-to-door salesman, and whatever self-respect he had was quickly evaporating because he couldn't seem to make a sale.

In one episode of the show, Dr. Hartley (Newhart) decided to go with him on his rounds, to see if he could help him grow in confidence and improve his sales techniques. So they went out, walking all over the city—only they never knocked on a single door.

When it was pointed out to him that he couldn't sell anything unless he knocked on a door or two, his reply was that he didn't need to knock on any doors because he knew nobody would want to buy anything from him anyway!

That's what I mean by saying that some people live their lives in such a way that they refuse to take anything but no for an answer. They approach everything they do in a negative, self-defeating manner.

"Shirley, you wouldn't want to go out with me, would you? No, I'm sure you wouldn't. Forget I even asked."

And meanwhile, Shirley hasn't said a word.

When you expect to be turned down, that's usually what will happen to you. When you present everything, including yourself, in a negative light, people will tend to start seeing you in a negative way.

So if you're living in a fantasyland that consists of anticipated rejection and failure, you must begin to make every effort to present yourself in a more positive light.

Don't say, "You wouldn't want to buy this widget from me, would you?" Instead, say, "Would you like to buy a widget?"

Don't say, "You probably wouldn't want to go out with me Saturday night, would you?" Instead, say, "Would you like to go to the movies Saturday night?"

Watch the words that come out of your mouth. Every time you hear yourself speaking in a negative way about yourself, make a mental note of it. Then, try to recast things in a positive manner. Every evening, go back over your day and see how many times you used words that tended to put a negative spin on what you wanted to do or say. Resolve that you will improve—that you will attempt to rid your vocabulary of words such as *can't*, *won't*, and *wouldn't*.

Then gather up your courage and start knocking on those doors.

You'll still hear a no once in a while—everyone does. But you won't hear it all the time.

4. Take a realistic look at yourself. Another way you can lower the high-jump bar of life is to see yourself as you really are. This is similar to learning to live in the real world, except that it centers wholly on who you are, what you can do, and how you fit into this world.

For instance, if you are a defeated perfectionist, you undoubtedly struggle with feelings of inadequacy. Does this make you a wimp or a weak person? Not at all.

Here is what the eminent psychologist Alfred Adler had to say:

> Everyone . . . has a feeling of inferiority. But the feeling of inferiority is not a disease; it is rather a stimulant to healthy, normal striving and development. It becomes a pathological condition only when the sense of inadequacy overwhelms the individual and, far from stimulating him to useful activity, makes him depressed and incapable of development.[14]

Did you read what he said? *Everyone* has a feeling of inferiority, so there is nothing at all wrong with you if you occasionally feel as if you don't measure up. When you come to understand that everyone you come in contact with feels that way too, to a certain extent, it can make you bolder and more self-confident.

I believe that most of us today—especially we Americans—tend to have a distorted image of ourselves because we are constantly bombarded by advertising, and because we live in a consumer-oriented society that tells us our worthiness is measured by how many "things" we can pile up.

I saw a bumper sticker not long ago which made me smile. It said, "The one who dies with the most toys wins."

Whoever wrote that bumper sticker had a lot of sense. What good do all our material possessions do us, especially in light of eternity? After all, we're not going to be able to take them with us when we go. And how sad that a man's worth should be measured by the things he has!

And what about the advertising messages that bombard us every day? We are taught that we're not successful unless we use this dandruff shampoo, that mouthwash, this other toothpaste, and wear clothes with the proper labels on them!

No wonder so many people feel that they can't measure up. They're never sure if they're doing everything they're supposed to do if they want to be popular and "together."

In one commercial, we are introduced to the sad plight of a beautiful woman: Some guy doesn't pay any attention to her, even though she's a stunning beauty, because she has dandruff.

Hey, let's face it. If the guy is not going to be interested in her simply because she has dandruff, he has much more of a problem than she does! So, some of the commercials are laughable, but others are subtler and are bound to hit home in varying degrees.

I make it a point to avoid buying certain products that use advertising campaigns based on snobbery, or the idea the you're not worth much as a human being if you don't use them. I also refuse to buy a certain brand of mouthwash because it is promoted by Dr. Phil. My feeling is that, my goodness, if we're taking advice from people like Dr. Phil, we're really in trouble!

And if it's not Dr. Phil pushing mouthwash, it's beautiful models with figures that must have been designed by Walt Disney (perfect, and too good to be true) or good-looking muscle men. The message the ordinary viewer gets is that he doesn't measure up if he doesn't use the products these people use—and beyond that he begins to feel as if he doesn't measure up anyway, because he doesn't look like one of these sculpted, chiseled specimens of human perfection!

Modern advertising techniques are thus used to sell us dozens of things we don't really need or want—or even know what to do with once we have them.

Now, I'm not knocking all advertising—just advertising that plays upon people's misconceptions about themselves and others. A problem for the defeated perfectionist is that he tends to believe a number of lies about himself, and this sort of "you're-no-good-unless-you-buy-my-product" advertising adds to and compounds those lies.

In *The Birth Order Book*, I talked about some of the lies we tend to believe about ourselves. These include: "I only count when I'm perfect." "I only count when I avoid conflict." "I only count when I'm noticed, and can be the center of attention." "I only count when I'm in control."[15]

Lies such as these are particularly dangerous because they contain the message that "I have to be doing something or acting in a certain way to have worth as a human being." The truth, though, is that I have worth simply because of the fact that I am a human being, created in the image of God!

You may also tell yourself these sorts of lies: "Nothing ever goes right for me." "I never do anything right." "Everybody else can do this, but I can't." If you're a parent, you may lie and tell yourself that all the other parents in the neighborhood are more capable and are doing a better job of raising their kids than you are yours. (And, if your kids are normal, they will be quite happy to add to that misconception. You know how it goes: Judy always gets to go out, so why should your daughter have to stay home? Tommy gets a bigger allowance, so why can't your son have more? Nancy's mother always helps her out with her science projects, so why won't you do the same? And on and on it goes.)

Don't believe these lies. Bad things don't *always* happen to you. You don't *always* goof up. The other people on the block aren't any more the superparents than you are . . . and on it goes.

If you are telling yourself lies like these, you're stepping on your self-esteem and holding yourself back. But you may be doing yourself an even greater injustice, and that is that you may be living a lie.

Do you find yourself trying hard to fit in with a group when you don't really care that much about the group to begin with? Do you put on a happy face and pretend to be a happy, contented person, when inside you really feel like crying? Do you find yourself spending time with people you don't really care that much about, just because you think it's the thing to do—or because you believe these are the sort of people with which you should associate?

Do you go around pretending to be something you really aren't or believe something you really don't, just because you know it's what other people expect of you?

If you do these things, you're telling yourself the worst possible kind of lie. You're saying, in essence, that our real self isn't good enough, that your real talents and desires don't measure up, that you aren't really acceptable, and so you have to put on a false face. If you're good enough at living a lie, you can fool just about everybody—with the one exception of yourself.

That gives you two problems. First of all, it lowers your self-esteem further, because you feel that your inadequacies have forced you to play games. And it makes you paranoid because you know that sooner or later the truth will come out. People will see you for who and what you really are.

What you fail to see is that people would like you every bit as much—and probably more—if they could see the real you.

Do you see yourself in this? Are you caught up in a life of lies? If so, it's time you began the process of lowering that high-jump bar of life by living your life the way you were meant to live it.

But how do you go about that? The first step is to try to be as honest with others as you can possibly be.

But I'm not talking about blunt frankness or verbal brutality. If Mary is wearing the worst-looking dress you've ever seen, there's no need to walk up to her and say, "What's going on, Mary? Dressed up for Halloween?"

I'm talking about a willingness to speak up for yourself, to express the way you really feel. It has to start with small things and carry over into the bigger areas of your life.

Suppose you've been to see a play at the local dinner theater, and you thought it was well acted and quite enjoyable. But a co-worker, who has also seen the play, says something to you along the lines of, "Wasn't that the dumbest thing you ever saw? I couldn't believe what a waste of time and money that thing was!"

How would you react? If you are the sort who tends to hide behind a life of lies, your tendency would be to say you agree with him. But if you are going to overcome and improve the way you feel about yourself, you need to tell the truth. Again, you don't have to tell your co-worker that he's crazy or that he must have missed the point. But you're going to feel a whole lot better about yourself if you say something like, "No . . . I didn't really feel that way. As a matter of fact, I enjoyed it."

There's no telling what he might say next, and if he's a particularly boorish person, there's a good chance he'll try to put you down: "What? You actually thought it was good? I can't believe that . . ." and so on.

But so what? As your mother used to say, "It won't kill you."

Sometimes we get ourselves in trouble because other people believe the lies we tell when we really don't want them to.

For instance, there was Juanita, a young woman with an extremely low sense of self-esteem. She was troubled by the fact that people never seemed to care about her or to be interested in her needs and desires. This was painfully illustrated by the fact that her birthday came and went every year without the other people in her office even mentioning it. In contrast to this, all of the other birthdays were celebrated with a lunch together at a nearby restaurant, flowers, balloons, cake—the whole works. Juanita tried to join in the fun and the celebration for the other people's birthdays, but her heart was never in it.

Why did the others always overlook her? Well, in talking about the situation, it came to light that she had always made a big point of insisting that she didn't want any fuss about her birthday.

When she had first come to work in the office, five years ago, the girls had listened to her say again and again that she didn't want them to celebrate her birthday, that she didn't like birthdays because they reminded her that she was growing older, and so on. They didn't know whether to believe her, so when her birthday rolled around, they put together their usual celebration.

Juanita's reaction was to act angry and pouty.

"I told you I didn't want you to do anything for my birthday," she fumed. Even though she really did appreciate it, she acted like she didn't. Her co-workers felt bad because they thought they had done something Juanita didn't want them to do, and they also felt slightly offended that their efforts were not appreciated. In the years since then, Juanita's "wishes" had been respected and her birthday was totally ignored.

Whenever one of the new employees mentioned that Juanita's birthday was coming up next week, one of the "old-timers" would say, "Oh, she hates birthdays."

Why did Juanita tell people she hated her birthday when she really felt bad when it was ignored? This was merely one of the lies she was living. It wasn't cool to want to be the center of attention. It wasn't right to want your friends to make a fuss over you. Then, too, she had such a low self-esteem that she figured people would forget her birthday, so she had to pretend she wanted them to.

The key, for Juanita, was to quit living a lie and to start being honest with herself and others.,

She wasn't able to start living an honest life overnight, and if this is a problem for you, neither will you. You won't always be able to say yes when you mean yes and no when you mean no. But keep on trying.

If this is a particular problem for you, you need to spend some time at the end of every day going back over the day's activities.

How many times did you try to perpetuate the lie? How many times did you pretend to feel a way you really didn't feel? How often did you say yes when you meant no and vice versa?

And as you are doing this, it is important that you are being as honest with yourself as you possibly can. Don't try to make excuses for yourself or pretend that you really wanted to react a certain way when you know deep down inside you didn't. If you are not totally honest and frank with yourself, you are not going to improve, and you are going to continue to go around on a treadmill of lies, pushing a wheelbarrow full of guilt and self-doubt.

In *How to Raise Your Self-Esteem*, Dr. Branden suggests the use of sentence-completion as a self-help technique.[16] One of his suggestions involves writing the sentence, "I like myself least when I . . ." and then filling in the blank. Add everything you can think of and be brutally honest with yourself.

Then do the same thing with "I like most when I. . . ."

This will give you a clearer insight into your own actions and motivations. When you give this type of thought to it, you can begin to see the ways you engage in self-defeating activities, and you can make a conscious effort to change.

Remember that you do not have to be what anyone else expects or wants you to be. You only have to be what you want yourself to be—who you really are. When you come to terms with that fact, you are taking a big step toward lowering your high-jump bar of life.

5. Face up to your fears. Are you afraid? Does it bother you and lower your self-esteem? Do you try to deny it?

Well, don't. Because the truth is, you're not alone in your fears. We are all afraid. My fears may not be the same as yours, but they are there nonetheless.

You may be afraid of the dark, whereas I may be afraid to speak in front of a large group. You may worry about the threat of nuclear war, while I worry about the stock market crashing.

You may be afraid that you're going to come down with an incurable disease, and I may worry that I'm going to be involved in an automobile accident.

But one way or another, we all have our doubts about the future, our worries, and our out-and-out fears.,

If you tell yourself you shouldn't be afraid, or that to fear something makes you a coward, then it's time for you to lower your expectations in that regard.

Very often, the person who has tendencies in the direction of defeated perfectionism has a problem with his fears. He tries to deny them and fight against them, which doesn't usually do any good at all, and then he berates himself for being a phony. He doesn't realize that courage really has nothing to do with the absence of fear. Ask some of the bravest heroes how they felt when they were performing their heroic deeds and they'll probably tell you they were scared to death.

The important thing is that they weren't immobilized by their fears.

If you've ever taken a Lamaze natural childbirth class, you know that one of the important aspects of this training is to learn to cope with the pain of giving birth. Pregnant women in this class are taught relaxation and breathing techniques to help them deal with the pain involved in contractions. I will never forget how, during the birth of our firstborn, I was holding Sande's hand and telling her that things were "fine!" "Well," she said, with an exasperated look on her face, "things might be fine up there, but they're not so fine down here!" But still, the idea behind this is a good one: If you tense up and fight against the pain, it's going to hurt even more, but if you can learn to relax and go with it, it won't hurt nearly as much.

It's that way with fear, too. If you tense up and fight it, chances are that it's really going to grab ahold of you. If you tell yourself things like, *Stop being afraid, stop having butterflies in the stomach,* and so on, you're probably going to aggravate things.

But, if you learn to admit that you're afraid, to go with it and accept it, you can overcome it.

You can even begin to talk yourself through it: "I'm afraid right now because I have to give a speech in front of the entire graduating class. It's perfectly normal for me to be afraid in this situation."

Analyze your fear and ask the question, "What's the worst thing that could happen to me in this situation?"

If you are about to give a speech, you might realize that the worst thing that could happen would be that you'd forget the speech, or say something that people didn't like, and you'd be embarrassed.

Well, that wouldn't be the end of the world.

If you begin to think yourself through the situation, chances are that your fears will begin to diminish. Perhaps you will even begin to laugh about them. For instance, if you were giving a speech, a statement such as, "I hope you can hear what I have to say above the sound of my knees knocking together," would be a good way to break the ice. It admits you're afraid, but it shows that you have accepted the fear, that you can laugh about it, and that you're going on with what you have to do in spite of it.

Fear is a natural part of human existence, so lower your high-jump bar of life and face up to your fears. Just don't let them immobilize you or lower your self-esteem.

6. Take responsibility for your actions. What's that? You ask how learning to take responsibility for your actions can help you lower your high-jump bar of life?

Simple. When you learn that you are responsible for what you do, and not for what anyone else says or does, you are freed from a trainload of guilt and worry. There is only one person whose behavior you can definitely change, and that is yourself. How your friends, relatives, and ultimately even your children act is out of your hands.

You are not responsible for the fact that your husband is in a bad mood because he had a rough day at work. You can sympathize with him, offer to give him a backrub, or do anything else you can to help him feel better, but you must remember that his grouchiness is not your fault. He has no right to take it out on you.

If Mary Anne wants to borrow your car, but you can't lend it to her because you need it today, it's not your fault if she becomes angry, or if she is inconvenienced.

Remember, you cannot be responsible for the happiness of other people. You can do your best to be sensitive to the needs and desires of others, but some people will not be happy no matter how much you do for them. If you decided you were responsible for their happiness, you could drive yourself completely up the nearest wall.

The reverse is true, too. No one is responsible for your well-being and happiness but yourself. To think that your happiness is dependent upon some other person—your husband, wife, mother, father, son, or daughter, or whomever—is to cop out and refuse to face up to your own responsibilities.

You mustn't go through life taking the blame for everything, nor can you go through life assessing blame for everything—or depending on others to fulfill your dreams.

Nathaniel Branden puts it this way:

Men and women who enjoy high self-esteem . . . take full responsibility for the attainment of their desires. They do not wait for others to fulfill their dreams.

If there is a problem, they ask, "What can I do about it? What avenues of action are possible to me?" They do not cry, "Someone's got to do something!" If something has gone wrong, they ask, "What did I overlook? Where did I miscalculate?" They do not indulge in orgies of blame.[17]

You may find it helpful to divide a sheet of paper in half and make two lists. On the left-hand side, write the things for which you are responsible. On the right, the things for which you are not responsible. On the left-hand side, you would place such things as:

The relationships I enter into.

The way I spend my time.

The amount of exercise I give my body.

The type of food I eat.

The way I treat other people.

My happiness or lack thereof.

And so on. On the other side, you would note that you are not responsible for:

My husband's grouchiness ever since he started work on the new project.

The rain last Saturday which spoiled the kids' plans.

The fact that Laura doesn't have a car.

And so on.

Again, I am not advocating that you abandon other people whenever they enter into a time of need. But there is a world of difference between trying to help them out and feeling responsible for their problems.

I know that life can be unfair and often is just that. Bad things may come your way in the form of accidents, diseases, or marital problems that you have not caused. But if you will take responsibility for your life, you are drastically improving your chances for happiness.

So remember that you are responsible for yourself, and only yourself, and lower that high-jump bar of life!

It's time you quit sabotaging your efforts. You'll never be perfect—but then, neither will anyone else. However, excellence is within your reach—and if you'll learn to aim for that, you'll be a championship high jumper in no time!

Promise Yourself You Won't Worry About:

What might happen tomorrow.

What happened years ago.

What others think of you.

Things you can't do anything about.

Whether you're going to fail.

What everybody else does.

7

Help and Healing
for Your Broken Heart

Amy had spent years looking for Mr. Right, but when she met Paul, she knew her search was over.

She had been in love before, but none of the relationships had lasted very long and none of them had ended by her choice. She was a warm, intelligent, pretty, blue-eyed blonde of thirty, who, for some reason she could not understand, was always getting dumped.

Somehow, though, she knew Paul was different. He was so strong, so pure in his motives toward her, and just so . . . right. She felt so happy when she was with him, and all her friends seemed to think they were made for each other.

What's more, Amy had a strong faith in God. She had prayed often that the Lord would send the right man into her life, and it was obvious to her that Paul was the answer to all of those prayers. This was especially evident in the fact that Paul was a believer, too, and every Sunday found them attending church together.

They had their fights, occasionally, but everyone has arguments now and then, and she never took them seriously.

Then one day Paul called her, and she could tell right away by the tone of his voice that something was wrong.

"Amy," he said, "I've been doing a lot of thinking about us. And, well . . . I just don't think we're right for each other."

She couldn't believe it. What on earth was he talking about?

"It just seems like we can't get along. I'm sorry, and I don't want to hurt you, but I just don't think we should see each other anymore."

Amy stood there in shock, staring at the receiver in her hand. After a good cry, she convinced herself that Paul would come around. Perhaps he was going through a temporary case of cold feet. After all, they were destined to be together. God wanted it that way.

But as the days, weeks, and then months passed by, it became obvious that Paul had meant what he said. He simply didn't want to see her anymore, didn't even want to talk about it, and his rejection was almost more than she could bear. She cried herself to sleep night after night and stumbled through her days as if she were a zombie . . . doing what she had to do, but without emotion or enthusiasm. She felt that she had been abandoned not only by Paul, but by God Himself.

Alan was a disc jockey for a country music radio station. He knew that the station's ratings weren't that high, and he also knew that radio isn't the most stable profession in terms of job security.

When he and his wife, Bonnie, had a chance to buy the house of their dreams, he wasn't sure whether it would be wise to make that kind of commitment. He decided to go in for a chat with the program director and lay everything on the table.

"Don't you worry about it," he was told. "Our ratings haven't been great, but they're improving . . . and the ownership is really committed to this format. We think it's only a matter of time before we're one of the top stations in this market."

The program director also had some nice words to say about the job Alan was doing and told him not to think twice about signing a contract on the house.

Exactly one month later—two days after Alan and Bonnie went through closing—he was called into a meeting where the station's staff were told that the station was changing formats. Country music was out, talk shows and news were in—and all the disc jockeys would be forced out of their jobs within the next thirty days.

Alan couldn't believe it. He had given his very best to the station, and this was how they repaid him. Why couldn't they at least have been honest with him when he asked them about his future there? But then, as far as Alan was concerned, this was merely another in a long list of rejections, disappointments, and knives in the back.

Amy and Alan. Two people who experienced severe rejection. Two people who discovered firsthand that life is often unfair and that your dreams don't always come true.

What about you? Maybe you've never suffered the devastation of being rejected by someone you love very much. Perhaps you've never been fired from a job. But to live as a human being is to be subjected to failure and rejection, no matter who you are, or how closely you guard your heart. Rejection cuts across all races, sexes, ages, religions, and cultures. Some are rejected by their parents, and others by their children. Some people are rejected by friends, some by lovers, and others by their bosses or their co-workers.

It's never easy to overcome rejection. No matter how much you may smile and tell people it really didn't hurt you, there's no denying the pain you feel.

I wish I knew of some magic formula, a few words you could say, or a special prayer that would immediately heal the pain of a broken heart. Unfortunately, I don't know of any. I know how bad the hurt can be, and how long it can go on.

But even though I don't know an instantaneous, magical cure, I do know there are some things you can do that will make the pain worse. There are also some things you can do to get through the worst of the pain, and steps you can take to rebuild your life.

If you are a person who tends toward defeated perfectionism, whenever you suffer a heartbreaking rejection, you most likely begin doing things that make you feel even worse.

1. You blame yourself.
2. You overgeneralize
3. You are so afraid of being hurt again that you put up a wall around yourself.
4. You look at the situation through the heart instead of through the mind.

Consider Amy, for example. When her relationship with Paul ended, she went through a long period of self-analysis, during which she thought about all of the things she had done that drove Paul away. This was her "if-only-I'd" stage.

Another thing she did that added to her pain was to look back over her past experiences, telling herself, "This always happens to me. I'll never find the right man." She also built a wall around herself, insisting that she would stay single for the rest of her life. And last, she refused to give the situation a good, hard look. Had she done so, she might have seen that what Paul was saying was really true. Their personalities didn't seem to be compatible. They spent much of their time together arguing and finding fault with each other.

But instead of thinking about all the times their dates had ended in shouting matches, Amy was dwelling on all the happy, romantic moments together. She totally idealized the situation and believed that when Paul walked out the door her world had fallen apart.

When you feel that you've been rejected, it's easy to fall into the same pattern Amy fell into. It happened to Alan, too. Now, I'm not saying that these people had trivial problems. They had serious, painful disruptions in their lives, and they were not helped by those who told them to keep their chins up and keep smiling.

Nothing can be more aggravating than well-meaning friends who think it will help you to hear such advice as, "You'll get over it," or, "God must really love you to let you suffer like this." I've been on the receiving end of such advice, and I'm sure you have, too. In order to get over a particularly painful rejection, you must do the opposite of everything Amy did. In other words:

1. Don't blame yourself.
2. Don't overgeneralize.
3. Don't build a wall around yourself.
4. Learn to look at the situation in the cold, clear light of reason.

Let me explain further:

1. Don't blame yourself. I know you've heard it time and time again, "Don't cry over spilled milk." Old advice. But *good* advice.

Three little words you should never say to yourself are *If only I. . . .*

"*If only I* had treated him better he would have stayed with me."

"*If only I* had let her know how much I cared, I know she'd still be with me."

"*If only I* were better looking, or more fun to be with, or a better dancer, or had more money (or a thousand other things), I know this person never would have done this to me."

How do you know you could have done anything to prevent the rejection from occurring? I have counseled many people who did everything they could do and still wound up being hurt and rejected. Some women have done everything they could do to keep themselves in shape. They've dyed their hair to suit their man's preference. They've learned everything they could about football because they wanted to share this part of life with him. They've gone on hunting and fishing trips, putting up with mosquitoes and cooking over campfires so they could be better companions. Some have even engaged in "wife-swapping" parties—not because they wanted to, but because it was what their husbands wanted them to do.

And in the end, after they've done all of that—even after they've debased and humiliated themselves—they've been rejected and abandoned.

I remember Audrey, a bright and attractive woman who dropped out of college and got a job so she could help her husband get through school. They struggled for years while he got a degree in pre-law and then went on to get his law degree. Finally, he was accepted into a successful practice and began making decent money. At last, Audrey was going to reap the benefits of her dedication and support.

But less than a year later, her husband announced that he was leaving her. He had fallen in love with another woman, a shapely blonde who was five years younger than Audrey. All those years of struggling weren't over after all—only now there was no purpose to her struggling, no looking forward to "better days" just around the corner.

So Audrey sat and played the "if only I'd" game.

It was totally ridiculous, because she couldn't have done a single thing more than she had already done for this ungrateful and unprincipled man. She could have wrapped up all the gold in Fort Knox, given it to him as a present, and it still wouldn't have been enough!

Audrey had a right to be hurt. She had a right to be angry. But she had no right to blame herself and play the "if only I'd" game. The problem wasn't with her; it was with her husband—but she had a terrible time seeing the truth.

I'm not saying that you shouldn't look back over what you've done and see if you contributed to the problem. That's being responsible. But there is a great deal of difference between demonstrating a responsible attitude and blaming yourself.

You're being responsible when you look back over the situation and ask, "Did I do anything that helped to bring about this situation?" It's not being responsible to say, "It's all my fault."

It's being responsible if you say, "I see where I made some wrong choices, and I want to learn from those so I don't make the same mistakes next time." It's not responsible to say, "I'm just no good at anything, and there's nothing I can do about it."

It's being responsible to have hope for a better tomorrow. It's not responsible to fall into a pit of hopelessness and despair.

I have counseled women who have been battered and beaten by abusive husbands, and yet they played the "if only I'd" game to the extent where they felt responsible for these attacks by their husbands.

"I guess I feel like he's right to hit me," one woman said, while she sat and nursed a badly swollen lip.

Incredible! Her husband was a monster, but she had such a poor self-image that she was ready to take the blame for anything and everything he did! And no woman *ever* deserves to be hit, slapped, or pushed around.

I also find that women who are sexually abused often tend to blame themselves.

"Maybe I led him on," they'll tell me.

"How did you do that?"

"I'm not really sure . . . but I must have."

She knows that she didn't do anything intentional. And deep down inside, I'm sure she knows that she didn't do anything at all. But she is almost convinced that merely being a woman is enough to drive a man to rape and brutality. Some women feel guilty simply because they are female.

This is true, too, of girls who have been molested by their fathers, uncles, or older brothers. As far as I am concerned, this is the worst type of rejection anyone could experience.

What kind of trust does a little girl place in her father? When she's two years old, he can put her up on a ladder and say, "Come on, honey, jump and I'll catch you," and chances are that she'll do it without a second thought. She trusts him and knows that he would never allow her to be hurt.

But when a father is molesting his daughter, he's letting that little girl hit the floor, and the injury that results can be devastating.

Let me add right here that I have learned to ask my female clients, "When were you first molested?" It really is that common. For that reason, I believe this is a subject that deserves greater discussion.

Perhaps you, yourself, were or are a victim of such abuse. If you are, you must remember that it is not your fault.

It's easy for a defeated perfectionist to take the blame. It comes natural to him. It's much harder for him to realize that other people are at fault and must be held accountable. But the very last thing you need piled on top of everything else is a heaping helping of self-blame. What you need to do is to figure out what part of the blame is yours—and perhaps it's as simple as being quiet about it and not telling anyone what's going on—and then acting to change things.

It could be that you are a woman who was molested many years ago, and all this time you've been carrying around a ten-ton weight of guilt and shame. If so, it's about time you took steps to forgive yourself for what happened to you. You may think your rage is directed at your father, your uncle, or whomever it may have been who molested you. But if you'll look deep down into your heart, you may see that you've saved the biggest piece of the blame-berry pie for yourself. So forgive yourself, find a qualified therapist to talk to, and take steps to change your life for the better.

Whatever type of rejection you have encountered, whether from a sexually abusive parent, an unfaithful lover, a boss who couldn't be satisfied, or an ungrateful child, you must not take all the blame upon your shoulders.

2. Don't overgeneralize. What does the defeated perfectionist tell himself when he goes through the breakup of a romantic relationship? Things like:

"I'll never be able to find someone to really love me."

"I'll always be lonely."

"No one could love me because I'm so ugly."

This last line has many variations, of course. You can replace the words *so ugly* with any number of substitutes such as "so short," "so fat," "so poor," "so uneducated."

And I will grant you that there may be many people who are better looking than you. There may be thousands of men and women out there who are taller than you, thinner than you, richer than you, and better educated than you.

So what?

There are more than 5 billion people in the world, and I would say that's pretty good odds against being the best in the world in just about any category!

But the reverse is true, too. With that many people in the world, you're not likely to be the worst at anything either. (If you were, you could really take pride in it, because it would be quite an accomplishment!)

But let me tell you how the defeated perfectionist tends to overgeneralize and overreact when he is rejected.

Suppose you're a young man who has just been dumped by the girl of your dreams. She was your ideal in every way, and you were looking forward to spending the rest of your life with her. You were sure that she was in love with you, too, and never doubted for a minute that she would quickly say yes when you asked her to marry you.

But when the big moment came—candlelight dinner, strolling violinist, everything exactly as it ought to be—and you popped the big question, she sat there looking at you with a shocked expression on her face. The minute you asked her, you wished you could take it all back, because you saw in her eyes that you had been a fool.

"Oh, Larry," she begins. "I really do like you—a lot. . . ." When she said that, you knew what was coming next. It was the speech about you being such a good guy, and how you'll make some "lucky" girl a wonderful husband, and so on—but how she's always considered you a "good" friend.

The more she tries to console you, the more you feel yourself shrinking away. You would love to be able to just disappear into the wallpaper, but of course you can't.

When the disastrous evening is finally over, and you're home with your thoughts, you stand analyzing yourself in the mirror, trying to figure out what is wrong with you.

All of a sudden you wonder how you could have ever believed that such a beautiful girl would want to spend the rest of her life with you.

Just look at the way your ears stick out. *Dumbo doesn't have anything on me*, you think. *And look at this nose. Jimmy Durante had a pug nose compared to me. And how come I never noticed that my eyes don't match. They look lopsided to me.*

You've never really given it much thought before, but all of a sudden you realize that you are one of the homeliest guys you've ever seen. No wonder she didn't want to marry you!

This is what Dr. David D. Burns refers to as "fortune-telling or mind reading."[1] How would you know why your marriage proposal was refused? Perhaps your intended just wasn't ready for marriage, or maybe she doesn't feel as if she could make you happy. Perhaps she sees differences between the two of you that you've overlooked because you've been riding along on emotional cruise-control and not looking at the situation with your mind.

There could literally be dozens of reasons why your proposal was rejected, and to say "It's because I'm so unattractive" is to overgeneralize and jump to conclusions.

To say, "I'll never be able to find someone to love me because I'm so unattractive," is wrong on two counts.

First of all because it's true that beauty is in the eye of the beholder. For instance, I remember Karen, who idolized her friend

Teresa. Teresa was so beautiful, Karen told me, that all the men went for her. Karen could see them turning to look at her when she went by. If only she could be more like Teresa.

Then one day I met Teresa. The experience was rather like going to see a movie that everyone has told you is going to be one of the best you've ever seen. Perhaps it's not polite, but I have to say it anyway: Teresa was a disappointment. She was tall, whereas Karen was just a little over five feet. She had long, straight blond hair, while Karen's hair was dark and naturally curly. But other than that, I really thought Karen was much prettier.

But there was something about Teresa just the same. She carried herself well, she smiled easily, and she exuded self-confidence. The difference between Teresa and Karen was that Teresa felt better about herself—period.

Later on, I told Karen that while Teresa was friendly, had a nice smile, and so forth, I thought she wasn't as attractive as Karen.

"What?" she said. "Oh, come on, you must be blind. She's beautiful!"

Beauty is a relative thing, and so is ugliness. One person may look at you and think you're the cutest thing he's ever seen in his life. The next person to see you may think you've been taking ugly pills. Do yourself a favor, though, and choose to believe the one who thinks you're beautiful! Who's to say he isn't right?

In his book *Intimate Connections*, Dr. Burns suggests keeping a scorecard on which you rate the couples you see according to appearance, each separately on a scale of one to ten. He believes, and I agree with him, that you're going to come to some interesting conclusions. For instance, you'll see a lot of threes and fours who are out with nines and tens.

In other words, you'll see some people who you think aren't particularly attractive, but they'll be arm-in-arm with some who are obviously of movie-star quality.

Says Burns, "This will make you aware of two old but very important concepts: Beauty is in the eye of the beholder, and there is more to forming relationships than just appearance."[2]

The second reason it's wrong to think *I'll never find someone to love me because I'm so unattractive* is because there isn't a person alive who could build a successful relationship with everyone he sees. Nobody bats 1.000.

As an example, consider the statistical charts compiled for major league baseball. If you notice that a guy *is* batting 1.000 (which is perfect), it tells you one very important thing about him—namely, that he hasn't been up to bat too many times. The same thing is true for someone who has a 1.000 fielding average. Either he doesn't get much of a chance to play, or he's not very aggressive in the field. A player who takes chances, who dives at balls he might just as well let go by, who charges hot grounders, and doesn't shy away from stinging line drives is going to have a few times when the ball bounces off his glove and he gets charged with an error. A player who doesn't do any more than is absolutely expected of him might have a better average—but he's not worth as much to his team.

Those who have never been rejected have never played the game. It happens to everyone, so don't tell yourself that something is wrong with you when you are rejected.

The defeated perfectionist always tends to think, when he has been rejected, that the person who rejected him was right. He needs to get to the point where he can believe that the person doing the rejecting may have been wrong, and that there is a distinct possibility that he or she will come to regret that action later on. (I'm not saying that he should overlook anything he has done to contribute to his rejection, but remember what I said about the difference between accepting responsibility and taking the blame.)

Whatever happens to you, stay away from saying *never, always*, and *I'm so. . . .* It's just not true, and it doesn't help you to think that way!

3. Don't build a wall around yourself. When Amy was hurt by Paul, she decided she would remain single for the rest of her life.

When I told her that she could get over the hurt if she would put her mind to it, and that she would most certainly be able to find a man who would truly love her, she looked at me with fire in her eyes.

"I will *never, ever,* allow myself to be hurt like this again!" She flung the words at me through clenched teeth, and I knew she meant what she said.

How unfortunate. Because here was a lovely woman—beautiful, loving, with a tremendous amount to offer the right man—but she was making it clear that she had already constructed a Great Wall of Amy around herself.

I wouldn't make light of Amy's pain, and I can understand how someone in her position would be afraid of being hurt again. After all, this wasn't the first time she had been hurt. But anyone who wants to live life to the fullest has to be vulnerable and take risks. It's ironic that some people tend to cut themselves off from others when they've been hurt, because this is really the time they most need the comfort that other people can give.

As far as I'm concerned, there are few things in life as important as lasting friendships. If you have one or two good friends, you should consider yourself a wealthy person. But to truly be a friend means to make yourself vulnerable.

The breakup of a romantic relationship is hard to handle, but in some ways, rejection or betrayal by a friend is even worse.

I have had people tell me that they lost their faith in God because of what a friend did to them. These are what I refer to as "pedestal people." They tend to idolize their friends, to see only good things about them. Then whenever that friend hurts them, whether intentionally or accidentally, they decide that they've been betrayed and want nothing more to do with the offending party.

Let me tell you something right now. If you have a friend who never, ever, lets you down, he's either a robot or you ought to start a movement to have him canonized.

People are fallible. People say and do things they don't mean. People get into bad moods or have bad days. Husbands let wives down, wives let husbands down, children let parents down, parents let children down—and on and on and on.

It's a good idea to know our own limitations and the limitations of others. Suppose you have a good friend, Myrtle, and although you love her dearly, you know for a fact that she can't keep a secret.

Then one day you find yourself saying to her, "Listen, Myrtle, I have to tell you something, but please don't tell another soul."

Well, of course she wants to say, "If it's that much of a secret, you'd better not tell me," but she can't do that because she wants so desperately to know this big secret of yours. So she says, "I promise." And you reveal to her one of the deep, dark secrets of your soul.

Myrtle honestly tries to keep her promise, but this forbidden knowledge is burning inside of her, and it isn't long before you run into Henrietta on the street and she says, "Oh, I hear . . ." and then proceeds to repeat your secret.

You might want to call Myrtle, chew her out, and tell her you never want to see her again. And, if you have a tendency to build that wall around yourself, you might say, 'I'll never, ever, trust anyone again. I'll just keep things to myself, mind my own business, and do without friends."

Now, I'll grant you that you weren't at all wise in sharing your secret with someone you knew to be a notorious blabbermouth. In fact, you'd be better off to be angry with yourself for telling her your secret in the first place.

Myrtle ought to be confronted about what she has done, and the situation must be dealt with. It shouldn't be allowed to fester, nor should it be used as an excuse to avoid being a friendly

214

person. (As in, "I know people think I'm cold and unfriendly, but I've been hurt, and I won't allow it to happen again.")

Don't put your friends and loved ones up there on that pedestal. They may have many wonderful qualities, but they are definitely not perfect!

When you've really been hurt, it's hard to talk to someone. If you're especially emotional, you might have trouble getting the words out, or you might say some things you'll regret later on. In a situation like that, I believe that writing a letter is a good idea—not a mean-spirited, name-calling letter, but a letter in which you explain your position and your feelings as clearly as you can.

You might say something like, "I'd like to talk with you, but I thought writing a letter would give me a chance to spell out what my feelings are. I'm really not happy with the way things are between us, and I want to work things out."

If your friend is any sort of a friend at all, he'll respond in a positive way. If he doesn't, and won't make any effort to resolve the situation, then you may be better off without him. But that doesn't mean you're better off without any friends at all.

Friends are extremely important. And if you have someone who believes in you, who encourages you, and listens to you when you're down, then do your very best to keep his friendship. But again, don't idolize him or try to make him believe you're something you're not. The best friends are those who are able to love you even when they must do it in spite of yourself, and the ones who are not afraid to show you their bad sides—warts and all—because they know your friendship is unconditional. As far as I am concerned, a true friend—someone you feel comfortable enough to be yourself with—is one of God's best gifts.

To build a wall around yourself, then, is to cut yourself off from potential friendships, and thus to refuse God's gift.

In *Intimate Connections*, Dr. Burns says, "If you're afraid of rejection, you need as much rejection experience as possible."

Although he is talking specifically to people who are looking for romantic relationships, his idea is sound for those who fear rejection in any way. He actually advocates collecting rejections. He teaches his clients to learn to smile and be friendly to strangers they meet. If they meet with a positive reaction, he advises them to take things a step further and ask for a date. Every rejection is worth one point. Once a client has received twenty points, he is to give himself a special treat like buying a new outfit he's had his eye on or going out for an expensive dinner.

He says, "Once you've been rejected a certain number of times, your fear of rejection will tend to go away because you'll discover that you do survive and the world really doesn't come to an end. As you become less and less afraid of rejection, you'll become more and more assertive and adventuresome. . . ."[3]

While I would not recommend that you go out of your way to seek rejection, his point is a good one. Rejection is not the end of the world, and the only way you can go through life without being rejected is to stay alone in your corner and not even try.

Consider the political career of Richard M. Nixon. In 1960 he was defeated in his bid for the presidency of the United States. Then in 1962, he was rejected again, this time by the voters of California, where he was running for governor.

But in 1968 he was back, this time winning the presidency, and in 1972 gaining reelection by a huge landslide. His career did not have a happy ending, of course, but nevertheless, his comeback election did demonstrate the fact that people can survive rejection and failure and come back stronger than ever.

So don't build a wall around yourself. When you do that, there's no telling what price you're paying.

4. Learn to look at the situation in the cold, clear light of reason. In their book *When Smart People Fail*, Carole Hyatt and Linda Gottlieb give what they believe to be the nine most common reasons people fail on the job. I believe their list is a good one and bears repeating:

1. *Poor Interpersonal Skills.* Do you have trouble getting along with other people? This is something which can be corrected. It involves learning to listen to other people, being sensitive to their desires, and so on. Basically, what this boils down to is having good manners.

2. *Wrong Fit.* It may be that your skills are not fitted for the job you are trying to do. This does not mark you as a failure but means that you should look for a position more in keeping with your abilities.

3. *Lack of Commitment.* Could it be that you are giving a half-hearted effort because you don't really believe in what you are doing?

4. *Bad Luck.* Sometimes things happen which are simply beyond your control. As I've said before, life is sometimes unfair, and the only thing you can do is dust yourself off and try again.

5. *Self-destructive Behavior.* This is often true of the defeated perfectionist, who sabotages his own efforts because he will never settle for anything less than perfection, but which he knows he cannot attain.

6. *Too Scattered to Focus.* some people are always biting off more than they can chew. They take on too many things to do any of them well and end up failing at all of them.

7. *Sexism, Ageism, Racism.* Sad but true that you may fall victim to the prejudices of others. But this has nothing to do with you as a person nor with your abilities.

8. *Poor Management.* You may fail because you do not possess proper management skills. But remember that good managers are made, not born.

9. *Hanging On.* Are you hanging on in a position, stagnating, when you really know it's time for you to move on?[4]

If you have suffered failure, whether on the job or in any other area of your life, it may be due to something you have done wrong, but then again it may be due to circumstances beyond your control. If the former is true, analyze what you did wrong and take steps to make sure you don't make the same mistake next time. If you did nothing wrong, but failure came your way anyhow, you must realize that these things have a way of coming out even, and you're overdue for a great big victory!

If you don't believe what I'm saying, just keep reading, because coming up next, I'll be telling you about some of the "biggest failures" who ever lived.

Part 3

No Losers in the Game of Life

8

A Few People
Who Didn't Measure Up

Let me tell you a little bit about a man who, by the time he was fifty years old, had failed in almost every way it's possible for man to fail.[1] Consider this:

When he was only twenty-two years old, a business he had started went broke. The following year he tried his hand at politics but was defeated in his attempt to win a seat in the state legislature. Then another attempt at starting a business failed. The following year, he finally won election to the state legislature, but his joy was short-lived, because a girl he was fond of became sick and died.

Even that terrible blow was not the last misfortune to come his way. He was later defeated in his bid to become speaker for the state legislature and in his attempt to become an elector. Twice he ran for the United States Congress and lost. Twice more he ran for a seat in the United States Senate, in 1855 and 1858, but was defeated both times.

Then he suffered another defeat, this time in his efforts to become the vice-president of the United States.

But he refused to fold his tent and spend the rest of his days in the never-never land of rejection.

And so, four years later, he became the president of the United States. His name, of course, was Abraham Lincoln, indisputably one of the greatest presidents our nation has ever had.

Have you suffered as many defeats and rejections as Abraham Lincoln encountered? I doubt it. I know that I surely haven't. Most of us would have decided that life just wasn't going to give us a break and given up. But not Abe Lincoln.

What a lesson his life gives to anyone who has encountered failure and rejection. You may lose battle after battle after battle, but that doesn't mean you are going to lose the war!

Now, there may be those reading this book who say, "Well, sure, everybody knows about Abraham Lincoln and how he bounced back from all those failures. But this is a really unique person we're talking about. He's a special case—an isolated incident."

If that's what you're thinking—you're wrong.

Albert Einstein found school intimidating and showed little aptitude for it. When he was fifteen years old, he left school briefly because he had extremely poor grades in his history, geography, and language courses.[2]

I can see it now: There's little Albert sitting in class, seemingly daydreaming, and doodling on a piece of paper.

"Albert! Albert!" Suddenly he's aware that the teacher is standing over him, glaring down at him.

"Y-yes, sir."

"The rest of us are conjugating these verbs. What are you doing?"

"Why nothing, sir."

At that, the teacher reaches down and angrily snatches the paper young Einstein has been "doodling" on. He picks it up and reads:

"E = MC squared. Now what in the world is this supposed to mean?"

Before his brilliant student can even answer he says, "I don't really care what it means. Just put this nonsense away and pay attention in class. How can you expect to be a success in life if you don't pay attention in school?"

And then, as my imagination shifts across the seas to he United States, I see another young boy sitting in class, absentmindedly drawing on a piece of paper. The student behind him pokes him in the arm.

"What is that supposed to be?" He points to the drawing of a little floppy-eared dog sitting in front of some sort of strange contraption with a big horn coming out of it.

"Oh, it's just something I've been thinking about." I call it a 'phonograph.'"

"Phonograph?" says his teacher, who's overheard. "Don't let me hear you say that again in my class or I'll wash your mouth out with soap!"

His fellow-student shakes his head. "You're really weird, Tom," he says and goes back to his math book.

I am referring, of course, to Thomas Alva Edison, one of the greatest inventors who ever lived and another person who bounced back from failure after failure. Young Edison was called "addlepated and retarded," by one of his teachers, who urged his father to withdraw him from school. He was considered a dunce by his neighbors, who often teased him because of his obvious lack of intelligence.

His father did not help the matter any, when he invited the whole town to come see him whip his son in the town square.[3]

This was a man who simply could not grasp Newtonian mathematics. He tried and tried, but it was beyond him. And yet he has some 1,093 patents to his name, including the phonograph, the electric light, the motion picture projector, and dozens of other electronic devices we take for granted as we use them every day.

You probably remember the old joke about Thomas Edison, where the teacher asked her students to write a theme about the contributions Thomas Edison had made to our society. "If it weren't for Thomas Edison," one boy wrote, "we'd all be watching television by candlelight." The young man obviously misunderstood Edison's contribution to twentieth-century life. Whatever you have around your house that runs on electricity probably was developed out of ideas first presented by Thomas Edison.

I don't know how you feel about it, but I'm awfully glad Thomas Edison didn't believe those folks who considered him a dunce and a failure.

He could have told himself, "They're right about me. I'm no good and I'll never amount to anything." But he didn't listen to them, he didn't give up when he failed, and he never stopped forging ahead.

Then, of course, you've probably never heard of a man named Winston Churchill. That's because his career was over and he was considered washed up way back in 1916. That was after he was blamed for two key allied failures in World War I and forced out of the admiralty. He felt disgraced and knew that his life of public service was over.

So what did he do after that? He became one of Britain's most dynamic, most effective prime ministers. His bold leadership and stirring oratory rallied his nation through the most desperate days of World War II, and he played a key role in his nation's government until the mid-fifties. In 1953 he won the Nobel Prize for literature—and he was also knighted and became Sir Winston Churchill. Not bad for a man who was disgraced and washed up nearly forty years earlier.

No, Abraham Lincoln was not an isolated case. In fact, when you really begin looking closely at the lives of famous people, you find that nearly all of them suffered rejection and failure at one time or another. Do you feel as if life has kicked you around and handed you more than your share of setbacks? Well, you ought to feel pretty good about the company you're keeping!

Could it be that failure is a prerequisite to overwhelming success? Obviously, that can be the case, especially if you will learn from your failures and seek to do things differently next time. Rejection can either weaken or strengthen you, depending upon how you handle it.

I've Been There

Now it's easy enough for me to talk about other people, but you can believe what I'm telling you because I've been there myself—and that means something.

Suppose you were planning a vacation and I told you to stay at a certain hotel because it featured fabulous rooms, the best food, and a stupendous view.

And then you asked me, "When did you stay there?"

"Well, actually, never, but I've heard about it."

If that happened, you probably wouldn't have a lot of faith in what I had to say. But if I told you I had stayed there on several occasions and had always had a marvelous time, then you would be more inclined to listen to me.

Well, I'm telling you now that I know what I'm talking about when I say that you can bounce back from rejection and failure because I've been there. I spent four years in high school just scraping by. And when I say scraping, I mean that I was really down there at the bottom of the barrel. I really didn't try, didn't see any need to try, and figured I didn't have much of a future to think about.

I was shaken out of my lethargy by a teacher who pulled me aside one afternoon and asked me, "When are you going to stop playing the game?"

"What game is that?" I asked, with a smart-alecky smile on my face.

"The game that you're the best at being the worst," she said.

225

I pretended to shrug it off, but her words hit home. I was bothered that this "old lady" could see through me and the game I was playing. She was the catalyst God used to get me moving in the right direction. I vowed that I would no longer let anything hold me back, whether it was fear of failure, a desire to be perfect, or anything else. But even then it was too late to do much about it in high school. I graduated very near the bottom of my class and had some difficulty finding a college that would accept me until I proved I could do better than my high school grades indicated.

Over the years, I have received numerous rejections, from publishers who didn't like my book ideas, from readers who didn't like the books after they were published, and so on. And I want you to know that I've saved every one of those rejections. Why? Because they provide the impetus to keep me going.

I look at them and I tell myself two things. First of all, that I'm going to succeed, no matter what the doomsayers may think. In other words, I've got the attitude that I'm going to "show them." Second, I vow that I will accept the valid criticisms and learn from those. I don't take all of the criticisms at face value, but neither do I disregard them all. I recognize that some of them are valid, but others are totally worthless, and I try as hard as I can to know which are which.

I appreciate people who bounce back from failure, who keep trying and never give up. I appreciate them because I know that, sooner or later, they're going to succeed.

I remember several years ago when a major league baseball pitcher by the name of Matt Keough was having an absolutely horrible year. Fifteen games in a row, poor Matt lost. But in spite of his incredible streak of bad luck, he kept his head held high, and he kept on pitching. If he pitched well, his team didn't score him any runs, but if his team scored for him, he couldn't seem to keep the other guys off the basepaths. It was one of the most incredible losing streaks I've ever seen.

And it wasn't a private affair, either. He tried to read headlines like, "Keough loses another one," and the whole world, or at least those millions of people who are baseball fans, knew all about it. Finally, that glorious day came when Matt Keough broke through and won his first game in sixteen tries. He didn't go on to win fifteen games in a row, or anything like that, but he did have a pretty good career. And he came out of the losing streak with his self-respect and his sense of humor intact. I admire Matt Keough for that.

Kurt Bavacqua is another baseball player I admire. Here's a man who was a marginal player. He didn't have overwhelming talent and he'll never be inducted into the Hall of Fame. But he hung in there year after year, made whatever contributions he could, and before his playing days were through, some seventeen major league teams were happy to have him on their rosters. I'm sure that during the length of his career there were coaches and fans who gave up on him, who figured he was washed up or that he couldn't contribute any longer, but time after time he came back and proved them wrong. He may not have had the greatest arm, or the best bat, but he did the best he could with the abilities he had, and they took him a long, long way. If you have the same attitude, it doesn't matter what others say, you can go a long, long way, too. You never have to settle for rejection and failure.

Let me tell you something else about rejection and failure. Some people are flat-out snobs, and they'll measure you by appearances instead of your innate worth as a person. Don't pay attention to those people—they're not worth it.

I learned this lesson when I was a student at the University of Arizona. To help pay my way through school I worked as a janitor in a Tucson hospital. There was one nurse in particular who didn't want to have anything to do with me. As a "common" janitor, I was beneath her, and she spared no effort in letting me know it. Whenever I tried to be friendly to her, I got no response at all.

I'd say, "Hi," whenever I happened to pass her in a hallway, but she wouldn't even turn to look at me.

At the time I was dating Sande, who would later become my wife, and this nurse simply could not figure out what Sande was doing with the likes of me. Obviously, my future consisted of pushing brooms or mops and keeping the porcelain in the restrooms bright and shiny.

At one point, this nurse even took Sande aside and advised her not to waste her time with me. Sande was pretty, intelligent, and certainly could do better than a janitor.

Well, naturally I was angry about that, but I didn't say anything because I needed the job, and I didn't want to make any waves.

But then one day I happened to wear a University of Arizona sweatshirt to work. For the first time I could remember, the nurse who didn't like janitors spoke to me.

When I passed her in the hall, she took one look at my sweatshirt.

"Why . . . uh . . . Kevin," I was surprised she knew my name, "are you attending the university?"

"Yes, I am."

She then proceeded to ask me all about my major, what field I was going into, and so on. She seemed, for the first time, to be genuinely interested in me as a person.

"Listen, Kevin . . . a group of us are getting together tonight— you know, it's Mary Lou's birthday. So why don't you join us? I'm sure it'll be a lot of fun."

You can bet that I didn't want to go. I was as polite as I could be, but inside I was seething. This woman didn't want anything to do with me when she thought I was going to be a janitor for the rest of my life, but things were different now that she knew I was going to be a psychologist.

I hope that if you push a broom for a living you will not misunderstand what I'm trying to say. I would never consider one person to be better than another, simply because of his job—but some people would. If you are a janitor, you enjoy being a janitor, and you're happy—then I'd say you're wildly successful. But there are others who are always trying to be a part of the "in" group.

Some people love to play one-upmanship games. You're not good enough because you don't have the right job, drive the right car, live in the right neighborhood, or have the right color of skin. Or perhaps you didn't go to the right schools, belong to the right social organizations, or even attend the right church.

If people reject you for any of those reasons, so what? You don't need those sort of people anyway. And who says that their definition of the "in" group is the correct one? Let them sit around and bore one another to death if they want to—you're better off without them!

I have very little tolerance or respect for people who delight in passing judgment on others. Just remember, if people are looking down their noses at you, the problem is theirs, and not yours!

Show 'Em They're Wrong

Your job, when that occurs, is to do your best to show the doubters that they're wrong about you. I'm not saying that you need to go around with a chip on your shoulder, with the intended purpose of putting people in their place. But at the same time, it's much healthier to have the attitude of *I'll show them a thing or two*, than to be thinking, *I'll bet they're right about me*.

If you're a sports fan, you've undoubtedly listened to Al Michaels, who is one of television's top sports announcers. In a four-month period during 1987–88, he announced the World Series, the Super Bowl, and the Winter Olympics. He's considered by many to be the top play-by-play announcer of the 1980's.

But he, too, remembers the times when he wasn't considered good enough for the job. In an interview with *USA Today's* Rudy Martzke, Michaels talked about the time he was rejected in his bid to become the announcer for the Chicago White Sox, and again for a football job with CBS-TV.

"Those things hurt, but I never lost confidence in myself," he said. And then he added, "I always felt as a teenager that if I got the right break, I would get to the top. If somebody doesn't think they're going to be good or get to the top, they'll never get there. I set goals, not only to be an announcer, but to be the best announcer."

Do you remember the Miracle Mets of 1969? The Mets, up until this time, had been a ragtag excuse for a major league baseball team. It looked like they had a lifetime lease on last place, and that they'd never be able to climb out of the cellar. And then, suddenly, they stopped being the team everybody else loved to beat up on, and started winning . . . and winning . . . and winning some more.

The players began to believe. The fans began to believe. Pretty soon just about everyone in the country believed, and the Mets went on to sweep past the Braves in the playoffs and polish off the Orioles in the World Series. The Mets were a good team that year—but really, not *that* good. How unlikely that a team that lost nearly one hundred games one year should come back and win one hundred, plus the World Series, the following year.

What did the prognosticators say at the beginning of 1969? They foresaw some improvement for the Mets, but not that much. Maybe they'd climb out of last place, but maybe they wouldn't. And then when the Mets surprised them by beginning to win, those who really "knew" about such things smiled and winked at each other and said it wouldn't last.

But through it all, the Mets kept believing—and kept right on winning. And that's exactly the attitude that you need to have. I don't care what anyone else says, you have to believe in yourself!

Another thing: I don't care who you are or what you've done, someone is going to put you down, but you don't have to listen to them.

Consider beautiful Kelly McGillis, the actress who has starred in such movies as *Top Gun*, *Witness*, and *Made in Heaven*. Despite all her current success, she remembers the pain of being rejected for a part in the 1984 movie *Bachelor Party*, because she wasn't pretty or sexy enough.

In an interview with Tom Green of *USA Today*, she said, "This is the head of 20th Century-Fox telling me I wasn't beautiful, that I'd never work in this business as an actress. I was depressed and suicidal. For about five months I couldn't go on an audition."

So, was the head of 20th Century-Fox right in his views about Kelly McGillis? Millions of movie fans will answer that question with an emphatic, "No!" Of course he wasn't right. And yet his rejection of her affected her deeply, and nearly derailed her career. Obviously, if an actress is too troubled by her looks to attend auditions, she's not going to get any roles.

Fortunately, Kelly's life changed when a director named Peter Wier saw her in a small role in *Reuben, Reuben*, and then cast her opposite Harrison Ford in the movie *Witness*. And since then, even though her career has taken off, she is still plagued with thoughts that she simply isn't pretty enough.

The actress also told Green that she was an overweight teen-ager who never dated and never dreamed of being a movie star. Green writes, "Her low self-image about her looks, she figures, may have drawn her to acting. She likes to change her look—most often to a new hair style or color, today blond and short."

That's because, in spite of all her success, she can't help but feel somehow that she's really rather homely.

Has anyone ever told you that you were ugly or stupid? If that's never happened to you, you must have lived your life in a vacuum. Perhaps it was your parents, or your brothers and sisters, or the other kids at school when you were a child. Did you believe them? The next time you see a movie with Kelly McGillis in it, just remember that she wasn't attractive enough to land that role in *Bachelor Party*. Seeing her up there on the screen certainly ought to make you feel better about yourself. I mean, if anyone has ever called you homely or ugly, you're in some pretty good company, let me tell you!

Have you ever watched or listened to children at play? If you have, you know it's enough to give you a renewed understanding of the concept of Original Sin.

I don't know why, but kids can often be terribly mean and cruel. They call each other names, they pick out the slightest flaws and magnify them, and they tease one another mercilessly. I honestly don't think there's a person alive who hasn't been subjected to this sort of treatment during his childhood years, whether from friends who were "just kidding," or from the "bad guys" over on the next block. Some people recognize this malicious kind of childishness for what it is, and they're able to let it bounce right off of them. But others, because they may have it reinforced at home or at school, tend to believe these terrible things they're hearing, and they're scarred for life.

I want you to pay really close attention to what I'm about to say:

I don't care what they called you, or what they said to you, it simply was not true. You do not have to believe it about yourself. You were not alone if you were subjected to this sort of ridicule and teasing. We have all been victims at one time or another!

I remember Barb, a very pretty young woman with beautiful gold-green eyes and silky blond hair, who sat with her head in her hands and cried, because she was so ugly.

She was beautiful, but she was a victim, primarily of her older sister who, for whatever reason (probably because she was jealous), constantly taunted and teased Barb about her looks. When Barb looked in the mirror, she didn't see reality. She saw a long, crooked nose, teeth that were too big, and skin that was flawed.

And Steven, who spoke of how ashamed he was because he came from a family of overachievers, and just couldn't measure up to their expectations. He didn't quite know why, but he just hadn't been blessed with the brains God had given to his brothers and sisters. I could tell, by just talking to him what an intelligent young man he was. But years of being put down and laughed at, of being called a "dummy" for making the same simple mistakes that every child makes, had taken their toll on him. He just knew he was stupid and fell apart whenever he was faced with the simplest task. He, too, was a victim.

Then there was Katie, an unhappy young woman who felt inferior simply because of the fact that she was born female. She was the victim of her older brother who never quit telling her that she was inferior because she was just a "stupid girl," that girls were worthless, and so on. Because of this, she saw every feminine characteristic within her—her sensitivity, her gentleness, her compassion for others—as signs of weakness and hated herself for them.

So you see, people can find fault with you for any reason. Some people, it seems, have dedicated their lives to criticizing faults in others.

But whenever you are victimized by such people, or whenever your best efforts aren't good enough, I want you to remember a few of your fellow human beings who were also viciously criticized and who suffered rejection and failure: Men like Abraham Lincoln, Thomas Edison, Albert Einstein, and Winston Churchill.

Yes, sir. The next time somebody tells you that something you did wasn't good enough or puts you down in any way, just lift your head and remember—you're keeping some mighty fine company!

9

It's Great Being You!

There are many times when I particularly feel a sense of awe regarding the glory of God and of the creature He has created in His own image—man (Gen. 1:27)! As you know by now, I have five children—five wonderful children if you'll allow me a moment of fatherly honesty—and seeing them come into the world and then watching them as they grow has been a profoundly moving experience. How anyone can consider the miracle of new life coming into existence and continue to be an agnostic or an atheist is beyond me! There is simply no way for this miracle of creation to occur without a great, wise, and loving mind behind it.

But there are two other specific times when I am overwhelmed by the fact that each person, among the more than 5 billion human beings on this planet, has his own unique design and character.

The first of these occasions is when it's snowing. Now, admittedly, we don't get a whole lot of snow in Tucson. We did get about four inches on Christmas Eve 1987, and the entire city was bonkers. When the snow started falling in Tucson, we thought at first that it must be the blossoms from the cottonwood trees. It was only when it started to stick, and when we discovered that, yes, it was slippery and cold instead of soft and fluffy, that we were able to admit that we were experiencing an honest-to-goodness snowfall.

But I haven't lived in Tucson all my life, and I still remember those winters in upstate New York, when you sometimes had to shovel your way out of the house in the morning—and then back in to the house in the evening. I remember how it was when everything in the entire neighborhood was covered in a thick blanket of snow and there was nothing but white as far as you could see. I also remember playing outside while the snow was swirling down, trying to catch the flakes on my tongue, and studying the huge flakes that fell onto my mittens.

I was fascinated then, just as I'm fascinated now, by the fact that no two snowflakes are alike. Each has its own particular identity. Tons and tons of snow, but all of it made up of tiny, little flakes, each with its own unique and beautiful design. When I consider that, I am overwhelmed by the design that God has built into His creation.

Now, a second time I am reminded of such things is, believe it or not, when I'm stuck in a traffic jam. I can already hear you asking, "What in the world could be awe-inspiring about a traffic jam?" I'll tell you.

I travel a lot, and because of this, I've been stuck in some of the world's most incredible traffic jams. If you've never driven in rush-hour traffic on the Harbor Freeway in Los Angeles, I'd have to say you probably don't know what a real traffic jam is like! I sit there, on what is supposed to be a freeway but is instead a gigantic ribbon-shaped parking lot. I'm not moving, and neither is anyone else, and I look around me. There's a guy in the far lane leaning on his horn, although what good he thinks that will do him I'll never know. A guy just ahead of me is pounding on his steering wheel, but the woman across from me is smiling and peaceful, undoubtedly listening to beautiful music on her car radio. On the other side of me, a guy is taking quick glimpses at his evening newspaper. Not too safe, for sure, but he's trying to make the most of his time!

All up and down the freeway, there are thousands of people, all with their own distinct personalities, all with their own private thoughts, all trying to get home to their wives, husbands, and children. Thinking about all of this is like thinking about the snowflakes, and it always makes me marvel at the uniqueness God has built into every human being.

It's easy, when you're stuck in a traffic jam or sitting in a huge crowd at a sporting event, to look around and see nothing but a multitude of generic people. But it really isn't that way. Just think of all the hopes, dreams, and experiences that each one of those people has had in his or her life. There are more than 5 billion people in the world, and no two of them are alike.

I am always amazed, for instance, by the innate differences among my children. They are all so different from one another, and all so different from Sande and me. I'm sure that any parent will tell you the same about his children. It's another evidence of the uniqueness of every human being, including you. You are not just an automaton, one of thousands rushed off the same assembly line. God made you to be something very special, a one-of-a-kind creation.

Look at the tips of your fingers and see the patterns in your skin. Think about the fact that nobody else in the whole world has those same fingerprints. Now, I don't believe for a minute that giving us each our own set of fingerprints was something God thought up just because He wanted to help to the police department or the FBI! I'm sure that any of us who have had our homes burgled have been grateful that fingerprints can be used to track down criminals—but that's not why we have them. We have unique fingerprints simply because we are—every one of us—unique creations of God.

And just as you have your own set of fingerprints, you have your own unique combination of talent, ability, intelligence, and personality. Nobody else knows all the things you know. Nobody else has felt all the things you've felt or thought of all the things you think of. Nobody else has had the same experiences you've had. And, I believe that nobody else can do the things that you are destined to do in this world.

You Are Making a Difference!

Some people get so down on themselves that they start to look upon themselves as expendable. "Nobody would miss me if I just went away," they think. "I'm just no good for anything!"

WRONG!

You'll never know how much impact you are having on the world around you.

Have you ever seen the movie *It's a Wonderful Life,* starring Jimmy Stewart? I'm sure you probably have. But if you haven't, or if you haven't seen it in a while, make a point of watching it the next time it's on TV. This is the story of a man who thinks things would be much better off for all concerned if he had never been born. And so, a friendly angel comes along and gives him a chance to see for himself. All of a sudden, his friends and family members no longer recognize him. What's more, they're not at all the fine people he has always known. He discovers, before the movie comes to its tearful conclusion, that his life has made a difference—a tremendous difference.

Some people are bound to say, "So what? It was only a movie—a fantasy."

Yes, but it is true that art imitates life. Your life *has* made a difference, and it will continue to make a difference. It may be your destiny to do some things that seem very small and insignificant to you, but which will have a profound effect on other people's lives. You may be the one who delivers an encouraging word exactly when it's needed so that someone else is inspired to become a leader for the nation. Your kind word or smiling face may save someone else's life. Your child may be a scientist who discovers a cure for some dreaded disease or comes up with a plan for ending worldwide hunger. What I'm saying is that you never know what sort of impact you're having on the world around you. Contributions that seem quite small to you may have a profound impact.

I recently came across an article about honeybees and, specifically, all the things that go into making honey. I've never really given a lot of thought to how bees go about making the stuff, I enjoy spreading it on a biscuit now and then, but that was about the extent of my knowledge.

I was surprised to find out how much is involved in the manufacturing process. First of all, several bees go out from the hive in search of the necessary flowers. When one of the bees finds a suitable field of flowers, he buzzes back to the hive as fast as his little wings can carry him. As soon as he arrives, he goes into a frantic dance that gives his important message, "Hey, guys, I found the perfect spot!"

He relays a variety of information through the way he dances, how fast he vibrates his wings, the direction in which he turns circles, and so on. From these signals, the other bees know how far the flowers are, which direction they're in, and something of the size of the flower field the "scout" has found.

As soon as the other bees have all of this information, they swarm out of the hive heading for the flowers, and the promise of the tasty honey that the community will soon be enjoying.

Now how did that first little bee know how to communicate all of that information? How did the other members of the hive understand what he was saying? How do they find their way to the flowers and then back to the hive in the first place?

The simple answer is that God has placed this information within them. The bee is not thinking, *Well, the flowers were a mile and a half to the northeast, so I have to turn in this direction now.* He does it simply because God has placed somewhere within him the instinct to do his dance in the right way. And the result of all this is some delicious and healthful honey for us human beings to spread on our biscuits. It's all a gift from God, and it's part of the unique grace and beauty He has built into His universe!

Have you ever heard a honking noise in the gray winter sky? You run outside in time to see a flock of geese, flying over in perfect V-formation, heading south for the season. Now, those geese hadn't been sitting around the lake in Canada talking to each other: "Hey, Ralph, don't you think it's about time we headed for Florida? After all, November's almost here."

"Y'know, Mabel, you're right. Time sure has a way of getting away from you, doesn't it? Hey . . . everybody! Listen up! Winter's moving in on us, so get a good night's sleep tonight, because we'll be heading south first thing in the morning."

And you don't find another goose saying, "Hey, Ralph, I think I'll pass up the trip this year. I'd kind of like to stay around and enjoy a white Christmas."

No, they don't need to talk about their pending trip or to debate the best route to take—they just know when and where to go. God has built the instinct into them, and so you'll see them flying south every winter to save themselves from the unbearable cold weather up north, and then you'll see them winging their way northward again every spring.

My belief is that just as God has built this knowledge into some of the lesser members of His creation, He has built special bits of knowledge, special abilities—given special gifts, you might say—to each one of us.

How do you go about finding those gifts and becoming the person God has meant for you to be? In his book *Confidence*, Alan Loy McGinnis lists seven specific things you can do.[1]

1. Focus on your positive qualities instead of your shortcomings. You do many things well, so why should you worry about the things you don't do well? If you can't play the piano, but you want to play the piano, then start taking piano lessons. There's no problem with wanting to improve yourself. But don't sit around brooding about the fact that you can't play the piano and letting your lack in this area eat away at you. If you took piano lessons and didn't do well, realize that this isn't your major area of ability and move on to something else!

I don't really know why, but it's true that most people want to be what they're not. If they're expert musicians they'd rather be superb athletes, if they're superb athletes they'd rather be expert musicians, and so the world goes round and round.

Some of you may be tired of hearing me talk about sports— but just one more time, okay? George Brett, former All-Star third baseman for the Kansas City Royals who was voted into the Major League Baseball Hall of Fame, was quoted as saying that he'd always wanted to be a National Football League quarterback. Chances are, if Brett had passed footballs for a living, he'd have said that he'd always wanted to be a third baseman. Strange but true that the other man's grass is always a tiny bit greener.

You must learn to take pride in what you can do well, instead of punishing yourself for what you can't do well.

2. Find your gifts and use them. As I've said before, all of us have certain innate abilities and aptitudes. Some people have known ever since they were small children what they wanted to be when they grew up. Very early in life, they'd displayed a talent for music, writing, acting, or what-have-you. Other people have never really known what their special gifts were, primarily because they've never looked for them.

But the key isn't necessarily in finding your special abilities. You can do that if you'll really think about your personality, what you like to do and don't like to do. (And I'm talking about abilities that range from being able to put other people at ease and make them feel at home all the way to a natural aptitude for understanding physics or genetics.)

The key is to use your talents once you've found them. You may have discovered very early in life that you had a natural ear for music. You could sit down at the piano and pick out just about any tune you'd just heard. But if that was all you ever did, if you never took steps to refine and polish your talent, you'd never get any better. When you were thirty years old, and by all rights should have been playing Tchaikovsky to a packed concert hall, you'd still be picking out "London Bridge Is Falling Down," with two fingers.

Whatever natural ability you have, it must be used, used, and used some more for you to develop it to the point where you're as good as you can be.

But the reverse is true, too. If you don't have any gift or ability in a certain area, then don't waste your time struggling along, feeling worse and worse about it.

It always upsets me when I see parents who insist that their child is going to take piano lessons—years and years of piano lessons—when after the first month or two of lessons it becomes apparent that the child has no aptitude for it at all. The poor child is developing ulcers, his piano teacher is about to pull her hair out, and the parents themselves are subjected to piano playing that sounds as if it is designed to accompany the yowling of cats on the back fence. And yet the parents will not give up.

How much better off for all concerned if they would realize, "This piano business must not be what little Elmo is cut out for. Perhaps we can find something else that he could do well, and that he'd enjoy, too."

If you're berating yourself for the things you can't do or because of who you're not, then you're simply wasting your time and being foolish. I guarantee you, whoever you are, that special abilities were built into you when you were created, but it's up to you to find them and use them.

3. Use positive self-talk. Who's your toughest critic? I wouldn't be a bit surprised if you are.

What do you tell yourself when you spill something on your favorite tie or blouse? Probably something like, *There I go again, isn't that just like me?*

What is your first thought when you're late for an important appointment? Do you tell yourself, *Why can't you get anywhere on time?*

And when you look in the mirror do you begin a barrage of self-criticisms? *Boy, your hair looks terrible today! Good grief, just look at that skin. Looks like you've eaten nothing but chocolate and potato chips for a week! Ugh! Just look at those wrinkles.*

Is that you? If it is, I have three important words for you: Cut it out!

In other words, stop being so hard on yourself. Give yourself a break now and then.

Stop expecting the worst to happen, and do your very best to think positive thoughts. There's no magic to it, but it's true that if you think better of yourself, you'll actually look better.

How do you react, for instance, when you look at yourself in the mirror and can't seem to find anything about your appearance that you like? First of all, you tend to slouch. Your shoulders droop, and the muscles in your face tighten because you're unhappy with yourself. Your attitude about your appearance will find its way into your arms and hands—you won't know what to do with them—and your voice will sound unnatural because your vocal cords are tight.

On the other hand, if you are happy with your appearance, you're going to stand up tall and erect, your arms will hang naturally at your sides, and your voice will be more appealing.

You may be objecting to what I'm saying because you think that being happy with your appearance isn't a matter of choice. But it is. You can make the conscious decision to center your thoughts on your good qualities, whether it's your nice smile, your eyes, your nose, or any other feature. Hold that pleasant thought in your mind. If you can't think of anything about yourself that you like, try visualizing yourself as you would like to be, and hold that image in your thoughts.

Then, learn to see yourself as successful. Those negative prophecies have been amazingly accurate. So will the positive ones.

4. Don't worry about what other people think of you. More specifically, don't try to be something that you aren't. Don't think that you always have to be the most intelligent person in the room, or the wittiest, the prettiest, or any other "est."

Do you have any friends who love to brag about themselves? It's an annoying habit, isn't it? And it's strange but true that people who do the most bragging are generally the ones who feel less secure in who they are. They're not content to be Joe Average and so they try to pass themselves off as Joe Superman. If you've ever spent much time with a person like that, you know how annoying and grating he can be.

So why does he do it? Because he is terribly concerned about what other people think. He wants them to think he's the funniest, smartest, handsomest, ad infinitum, ad nauseum. Especially the nauseum.

He hasn't learned that people tend to like you much more if you talk less about yourself and more about them.

Mary Lou felt terrible whenever she spent time with any of her husband's friends. Her husband was a well-read professional man with a master's degree from a prestigious university, whereas she had gone to a junior college for only one semester. She felt ill at ease whenever they would to go dinner with a circle of his "literate" friends and just knew they were looking down their noses at her.

She finally realized that she was so worried about making a good impression on them that she wasn't showing the least bit of interest in what they had to say. Instead, she was often monopolizing the conversation and attempting to discuss things she knew nothing about. When she changed her attitude, realized it was okay to admit her ignorance on some subjects, began asking questions, and giving other people the opportunity to talk about themselves, she suddenly began fitting in more easily. She discovered that people liked her for who she was—and not for who she wasn't.

If they didn't like her for who she was, that was their problem, and they weren't worth much as friends anyway.

Do you see yourself as plain vanilla in a tutti-frutti world? That could be true, but just remember that vanilla is still the most popular flavor!

5. Strengthen your friendships. I've talked before about the importance of good friends. It doesn't matter so much how many friends you have, but you need to have one or two good ones.

If you're like most modern Americans, chances are that you have dozens of acquaintances, but very few close friends. Perhaps you are spreading yourself too thin and trying too hard to get people to like you.

You're not going to get everybody in the world—or even in your neighborhood—to think you're a great person. But one or two close friends can be a tremendous source of strength and support. They can help you develop into the person God wants you to be.

As I said before, if you have a friend who really believes in you—warts and all—then hang on to him for all you're worth. If you don't have a friend like that, go out and find one.

How do you do that? You won't find him if you're sitting home watching "Wheel of Fortune" by yourself. Developing a good friendship takes effort, and the effort begins with meeting potential friends. Becoming involved in a church organization is a good way to start. It's been my experience that you'll find the nicest people inside the walls of the church. Civic and social organizations are good, too. There are dozens of ways to meet people who share your tastes and interests, but remember the old Muslim proverb: "If the mountain won't come to Moham-med, Mohammed will go to the mountain." If the people won't come traipsing through your living room, then you'll have to go to the people.

And once you've met these potential friends, talk to them. Show an interest in them, and chances are good that they will show an interest in you.

I'm not saying that you should zero in on some stranger and say, "Okay, this guy is going to be my best friend." If you do that, you've got a pretty good chance of picking out someone with whom you have absolutely nothing in common!

But if you learn to be friendly and just talk to people, soon you're going to find someone who's looking for a person just like you to be his friend.

This sounds pretty basic, I know. It may come across as some-what condescending or insulting. If it does, I ask your indulgence and forgiveness. But experience has shown me that there are many lonely people who don't have the slightest idea how to go about forming friendships. And that's a pity, because God has designed us humans with an innate need for fellowship.

You have to remember, too, that you have plenty to offer these potential friends, and if they don't ever get to know you, they're the ones who are missing out.

One last word about friendships: Don't play games like, "It's Mary's turn to call me, so I'm not going to call her," or, "I asked John to go to lunch with me last week, so it's his turn to call me. If he doesn't, we just won't get together."

That sort of halfhearted commitment to people isn't the max-imum effort that's required to build true and lasting friend-ships.

6. Develop the spiritual side of your life. I mentioned that getting involved in a church is a good way to find friends. There is one Friend in particular that church attendance can help you get to know better, and that's God.

Has it been a while since you've attended a worship service? Then why not make plans to be in church this weekend?

I sometimes counsel people who don't see any need to have God in their lives. They remember how close they felt to Him when they were children, how they talked to Him every day and knew He was there looking out for them. Now that they've grown up, they've set aside that relationship with the Creator of the universe as something that belonged to their childhood. Some of them are miserable people, but they fail to see that a large portion of that misery has to do with excluding God from their lives.

Too many people get confused about God. They start to believe He's like Santa Claus or the Easter Bunny—a nice story, but not real. But He is real, He is there, and He does care about the people He has created. Day after day, year after year, God proves His loving faithfulness to His people. If you don't see Him in your life anymore, it must be because you have your spiritual eyes closed. Because He's the One who designed you, He's the One who knows what you need to be a healthy, happy individual. And I don't care how contented someone may feel, unless God is a part of his life, he's missing out on something very important.

If you've drifted away from God, make efforts to renew that relationship. Start talking to Him. He'll listen. Tell Him all about your hopes and your troubles and ask Him to help you be the sort of person you'd like to be.

Thank Him for creating you and ask Him to help you remember that He doesn't make any mistakes. God is speaking to you, telling you that you are important because of who you are—a human being created in His image—and not because of what you own or what you've done. All human love contains an element of rejection, but God's love is offered freely and without condition.

Once you have deepened or reestablished your relationship with God, look for a church where you can fit in comfortably with the other believers—where there is an open, loving, affirming attitude.

I believe you can read all the books in the world, gather all the wisdom from the minds of great men, but if you still lack communication with your Creator you will continue to be victimized by uncertainty and self-doubt.

Every human being has a spiritual side, along with the physical and the emotional/mental. Do your best to stay physically fit, of course, and to increase your mental capacity. But if you're neglecting your spiritual side, you are out of balance.

7. Stop playing comparison games. You must realize that you are a unique individual. You're not like anyone else. You have your own special set of strengths and weaknesses that make you uniquely fitted to fulfill God's purpose for your life.

The old Indian proverb says not to judge another man until you have walked a mile in his moccasins. I would add to that and tell you not to envy another man until you have walked a mile in his moccasins.

Does it seem that he's so much better off than you? Chances are he isn't. He has troubles and fears that you can't see. Remember Edwin Arlington Robinson's poem about Richard Cory, the man who was the envy of everyone but who was so unhappy that he took his own life? You'll never know the hurts and pains of people like Richard Cory.

If you could change places with that man you envy, you would probably find yourself saying, "Boy, it was great being me!"

If you feel that you don't measure up, it's largely because you've been trained to feel bad about yourself. You have to change that attitude and see that you are just as good as anyone else on this planet.

Did you know that most people will weigh more a year after they go on their first diet? Why? Because they've attacked the symptoms rather than the root of the problem. The key to effective and permanent weight loss is to change your attitude about food—and learn to see eating as something you do to live, instead of the other way around.

Building self-esteem also takes a change of attitude. You can buy yourself a new suit, get your hair fixed, and your face made up—but it's not going to do you one bit of good until you change your attitude about yourself. But if you are willing to make the effort, you really can change things.

Now, reading this book isn't going to help you at all, unless you put the things you've learned into practice. If you put this book up on a shelf now and forget all about the things we've discussed, then you've been wasting your time.

But if you'll go back through it again and make your best effort to make the changes you need to make in your life, you're going to be amazed at what happens.

You spend priority time on everything else—getting the house fixed up, getting your body into shape, getting your lawn in order. So why not make yourself your number one priority for the next several months. No, not in a selfish way, but in the sense that you want to become everything you can be! You owe that to yourself, your friends, your family, and your Creator.

I invite you to make one of the greatest discoveries of your life: The discovery that it is great being you!

Notes

Chapter 1 Why Can't I Measure Up?

1. Quiz based on Dr. David Brandt, *Don't Stop Now You're Killing Me* (New York: Poseidon Press, 1986), 144–45.

Chapter 2 What's This Thing Called *Life-Style*?

1. Dr. Alfred Adler, *The Practice of Individual Psychology* (London: Routledge & Kegan Paul, 1923), 3.

2. See Leroy Baruth and Daniel Eckstein, *Lifestyle: Theory, Practice, and Research* (Dubuque, Ia.: Kendall/Hunt Publishing, 1978), 1–9.

3. Quoted in Heinz L. and Rowena R. Ansbacher, *The Individual Psychology of Alfred Adler* (New York: Harper & Row, 1964), 172–73.

Chapter 3 How the Pattern Begins: The Early Years

1. Dr. R. D. Coddington, "Life Events Scales for Adolescents and Children," in *Stress in Childhood*, ed. James H. Humphrey (New York: AMS Press, 1984), 102–5.

2. See Kevin Leman, *Making Children Mind without Losing Yours* (Old Tappan, N.J.: Revell, 1984), 127–29.

3. Dr. Ross Campbell, *How to Really Love Your Child* (Wheaton: Victor, 1981), 49,

4. Marie Winn, *The Plug-In Drug* (New York: Viking Books, 1985), 147.

5. Adapted from Leman, *Making Children Mind*, 130–33.

6. James Dobson, *Dare to Discipline* (Wheaton: Tyndale, 1978), 56.

7. Adapted from Leman, *Making Children Mind*, 158.

8. Ibid., 111.

9. Ibid., 88–89.

10. Ibid.

Chapter 4 The Critical Parent and You

1. See Kevin Leman, *The Pleasers: Women Who Can't Say No and the Men Who Control Them* (Old Tappan, N.J.: Revell, 1987).

2. George Orwell, *1984* (New York: Harcourt Brace Jovanovich, 1949).

Chapter 5 The Problem with Guilt

1. Quoted in Jane Goodsell, *Not a Good Word about Anybody* (New York: Ballantine Books, 1988), 95.

2. Statistics provided by the National Institute of Mental Health.

3. Adapted from Kevin Leman, *The Pleasers: Women Who Can't Say No and the Men Who Control Them* (Old Tappan, N.J.: Revell, 1987), 125–49.

4. Dr. David Burns, *Feeling Good* (New York: Signet Books, 1981), 178–79.

5. Adapted from Leman, *The Pleasers*, 147–49.

6. Dr. Gerald G. Jampolsky, *Goodbye to Guilt* (New York: Bantam Books, 1985), 33.

7. Ibid., 42.

8. Ibid., 32.

9. Leman, *The Pleasers*, 148.

10. Quoted in Goodsell, *Not a Good Word*, 83.

Chapter 6 Is It Time to Lower Your High-Jump Bar of Life?

1. See Kevin Leman, *The Birth Order Book* (Old Tappan, N.J.: Revell, 1985), 63.

2. The Doors, "The End" (Nipper Music, ASCAP, 1963).

3. Quoted in Jane Goodsell, *Not a Good Word about Anybody* (New York: Ballantine Books, 1988), 50.

4. Adapted from Leman, *Birth Order Book*, 70.

5. Paraphrased from Granland Rice, quoted in Bruce Bohle, *The Home Book of American Quotations* (New York: Dodd, Mead, 1967), 386.

6. It was Bill Veeck not Vince Lombardi who said this according to Bohle, *American Quotations*, 386.

7. Quoted in Carole Hyatt and Linda Gottlieb, *When Smart People Fail* (New York: Simon and Schuster, 1987), 34.

8. Ibid., 232–36.

9. Ibid., 38.

10. See Nathaniel Branden, *How to Raise Your Self-Esteem* (New York: Bantam Books, 1987), 27–43.

11. Ibid., 34.

12. Ibid., 40.

13. Quoted in Goodsell, *Not a Good Word*, 51.

14. Quoted in Heinz L. and Rowena R. Ansbacher, *The Individual Psychology of Alfred Adler* (New York: Harper & Row, 1964), 258.

15. See Leman, *Birth Order Book*, 112–25.

16. Branden, *How to Raise Your Self-Esteem*, 22–23.

17. Ibid., 109.

Chapter 7 Help and Healing for Your Broken Heart

1. David D. Burns, *Intimate Connections* (New York: Signet Books, 1985), 212.

2. Ibid., 93.

3. Ibid., 208.

4. Adapted from Carole Hyatt and Linda Gottlieb, *When Smart People Fail* (New York: Simon and Schuster, 1987), 103–30.

Chapter 8 A Few People Who Didn't Measure Up

1. Jeanne Larson and Ruth McLin, *Climbing Jacob's Ladder* (Washington, D.C.: Review and Herald Publishing, 1979), 26.

2. Milton Adams, *Albert Einstein* (New York: Franklin Watts, 1983), 3–12.

3. Jane Goodsell, *Not a Good Word about Anybody* (New York: Ballantine Books, 1988), 3.

Chapter 9 It's Great Being You!

1. Adapted from Alan Loy Mcginnis, *Confidence* (Minneapolis: Augsburg Publishing, 1987), 10.

Founder of matchwise.com, internationally known Christian psychologist, award-winning author, radio and television personality, and speaker, **Dr. Kevin Leman** has ministered to and entertained audiences worldwide with his wit and commonsense psychology.

Bestselling author Dr. Leman has made house calls for *Focus on the Family* with Dr. James Dobson as well as numerous radio and television programs, including *Oprah, American Morning,* CBS's *The Early Show, Today,* and *The View.* Dr. Leman has served as a consulting family psychologist to *Good Morning America.*

Dr. Leman is the founder and president of Couples of Promise, an organization designed and committed to helping couples remain happily married. His professional affiliations include the American Psychological Association, the American Federation of Radio and Television Artists, the National Register of Health Services Providers in Psychology, and the North American Society of Adlerian Psychology.

Dr. Leman attended North Park College. He received his bachelor's degree in psychology from the University of Arizona, where he later earned his master's and doctorate degrees. Originally from Williamsville, New York, he and his wife, Sande, live in Tucson, Arizona. They have five children and one grandchild.

For more information regarding speaking availability, business consultations, or seminars, please contact Dr. Leman at:

Dr. Kevin Leman
P.O. Box 35370
Tucson, Arizona 85740
Phone: (520) 797-3830
Fax: (520) 797-3809
Web site: www.realfamilies.com or www.matchwise.com